Keyboard Primer
with Video & Audio Access

by
Lee Davis

For Video & Audio Access, go to this internet address:
http://cvls.com/extras/keyboard/

Copyright 2017 by Watch & Learn, Inc. First Edition
ALL RIGHTS RESERVED. Any copying, arranging, or adapting of this work without the
consent of the owner is an infringement of copyright.

HOW TO USE THE

To use the *Keyboard Primer* book and Video together, follow these suggestions.

Step 1

Watch a section of the Video, then rewind and watch it again until you understand the material completely. (A section would be from one title page to the next).

Step 2

Once you understand the section, go to the book to practice the exercises and songs over and over until you are comfortable with them.

Step 3

After practicing with the book, go back to the Video and play along with it to make sure you are performing the material correctly.

This course is designed to be worked through, stopping and practicing each section until you are thoroughly familiar with the material. It will probably take the average beginning student 2 - 4 months to work all the way through the book and Video, so don't get in a hurry. Take your time and learn the material correctly.

The information in this book and Video combination is the result of over 20 years of studying and performing keyboards by Lee Davis, combined with over 60 years of teaching and publishing experience of the Watch & Learn staff. This information was gathered from Lee and organized by Peter Vogl, Bert Casey, and Geoff Hohwald. Peter and Bert in particular spent over 200 hours transcribing, recording, proof reading, and editing the *Keyboard Primer* to make this the finest and most accurate keyboard method available.

INTRODUCTION

The *Keyboard Primer with Video & Audio Access* will quickly transform you from an absolute beginner into a student/keyboardist with a full understanding of the fundamentals and techniques of playing the keyboard. This clear, step-by-step method includes many photographs, large easy-to-read notation, and a sequence of learning that has been meticulously developed and tested over a 20 year period. With each new song, you will learn new techniques to establish a firm foundation that will enable you to enjoy playing keyboards for many years. It's no wonder the *Keyboard Primer* is the first choice of over 2,000 stores throughout the United States and Canada.

The companion Video provides the accent, tone, and rhythm for all the songs and exercises in this book. This enables you to progress even faster because you will be able to see the correct movements of the left and right hand.

THE AUTHOR

Lee Davis is an Atlanta session musician and performer with over 20 years of experience playing and teaching keyboards. Lee performs nightly with some of the top acts in the South. He also does extensive recording work with MLD Productions and Maysville Music, and has recorded two solo CDs.

WATCH & LEARN PRODUCTS REALLY WORK

25 years ago, Watch & Learn revolutionized music instructional courses by developing well thought out, step-by-step instructional methods combined with clear, easy-to-understand graphics that were tested for effectiveness on beginners before publication. This concept, which has dramatically improved the understanding and success of beginning students, has evolved into the Watch & Learn mastermind of authors, editors, teachers, and artists that continue to set the standard of music instruction today. This has resulted in sales of almost 1.5 million products since 1979. This high quality course will significantly increase your success and enjoyment while playing the keyboard.

VIDEO & AUDIO ACCESS

For Audio & Video Access, go to this internet address:

http://cvls.com/extras/keyboard/

TABLE OF CONTENTS

SECTION 1   Page #
GETTING STARTED
- The Keyboard.................................1
- Cables & Amp 2
- Sitting Position...............................3
- Hand Position.................................4
- Learning The Keys..........................5
- A Beginning Exercise 8
- Left Hand Exercise 9
- Review 10

SECTION 2 - RHYTHM & NOTES
- Right Hand Etude..........................12
- Left Hand Reggae 13
- The Treble Clef 14
- Note Values 16
- Song For Right Hand 18
- Clair De Lune................................18
- Ode To Joy 19
- Simple Melody..............................19
- Mary Had A Little Lamb.................20
- Right Ahead 20
- Finger Ease 20
- The Bass Clef 21
- Song For The Left Hand 22
- Clair De Lune Bass Clef 23
- Steps 24
- Bass Clef Study 24
- Grand Staff Song 1........................25
- Grand Staff Song 2........................26
- Ode To Joy 27
- Major Melody 29

SECTION 3 - CHORDS   Page

- Chords 31
- Chord Song 33
- Chord Workout 34
- Inner Voices 34
- Chord Song/Bass Line 35
- Tom Dooley 36

SECTION 4 - C MAJOR SCALE

- C Major Scale/Right Hand 38
- C Major Scale/Left Hand 40
- C Major Song 42
- Two Hand Control 44
- Michael Row The Boat Ashore 45
- Yankee Doodle 46
- Oh Suzanna 47
- The Caissons Go Rolling Along 48
- Oh When The Saints 50
- Scaling Heights 51
- Interval Workout 52
- Twinkle, Twinkle Little Star 53
- Canon In C 54
- Thirds 57
- What To Do Next 58

SECTION 1
GETTING STARTED

For Audio & Video Access, go to this internet address:
http://cvls.com/extras/keyboard/

THE KEYBOARD

Top View of Keyboard

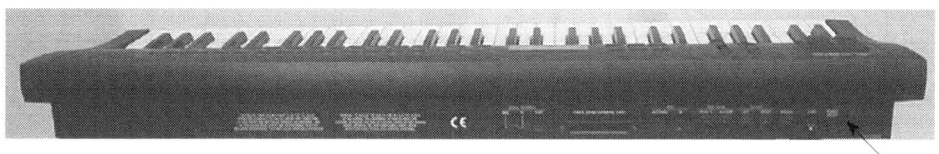

Back View of Keyboard

On-Off Switch

  For those of you with your very first keyboard, we will help you get started. If you are playing a piano, you may skip to page 3. Most keyboards have an on/off switch located on the back, either on the far right or far left. Locate the switch and turn it on. Many keyboards come with internal speakers so you can hear what you are playing. If your keyboard has no speakers, you'll need an amplifier and an instrument cable.

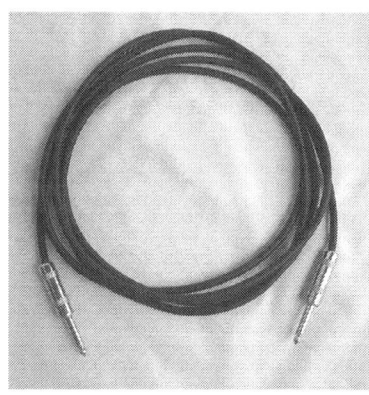

Cable

Amplifier

1

CABLES & AMP

Plug one end of the cable into the output jack of the keyboard and the other end into the input jack of the amplifier. Make sure the amp is turned off before you plug it in. Now turn on the amplifier and adjust the volume.

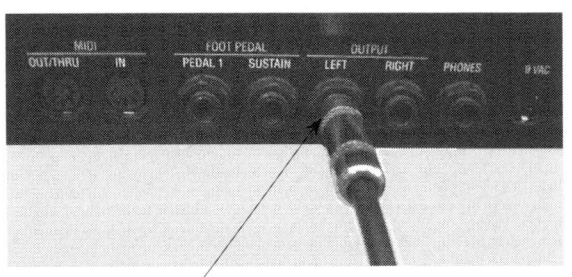

Cable inserted into back of Keyboard

Cable inserted into amp

Adjust Volume

In this course we'll use a piano sound. Most keyboards automatically select a piano sound when you turn it on. If it doesn't, scroll through the settings until you find the piano sound. There's also a volume control, usually located at the far left of the keyboard. If you aren't getting any sound and you are using an amp, make sure the volume knob on the amp is turned up.

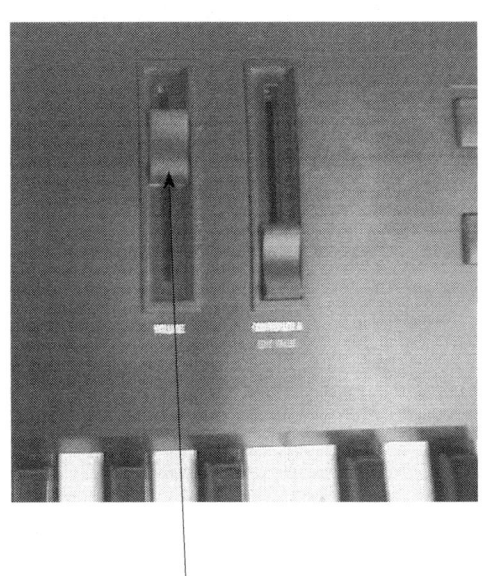

Keyboard Volume Control

Amplifier Volume Dial

SITTING POSITION

Your keyboard is best played on a stable keyboard stand. If you don't have a stand, you can purchase one at your local music store. The keyboard should be at a height just below your elbows when you are sitting. Adjust the stand to get the keyboard at the correct height. You will also need a comfortable chair and a music stand.

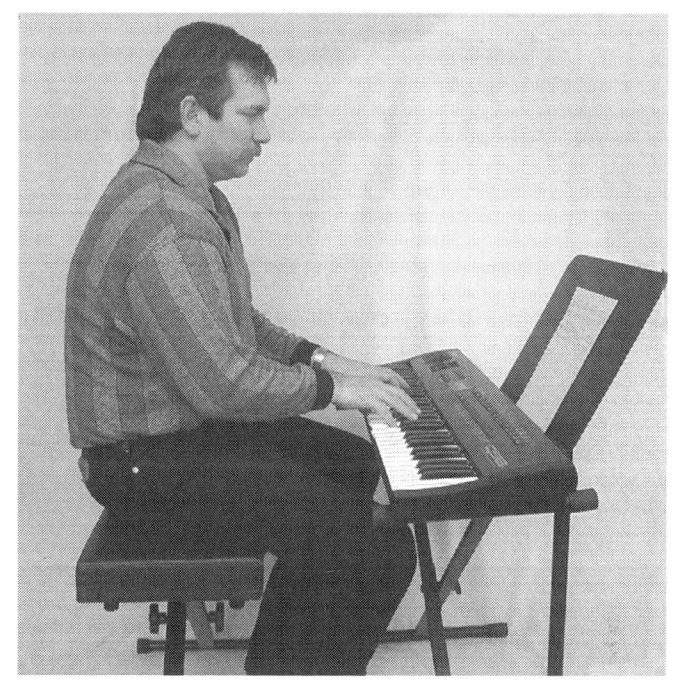

Sit up straight. Let your arms hang down freely, then raise your hands until they are parallel to the floor. Don't rest your arms on your knees when playing. Place your feet in a comfortable position.

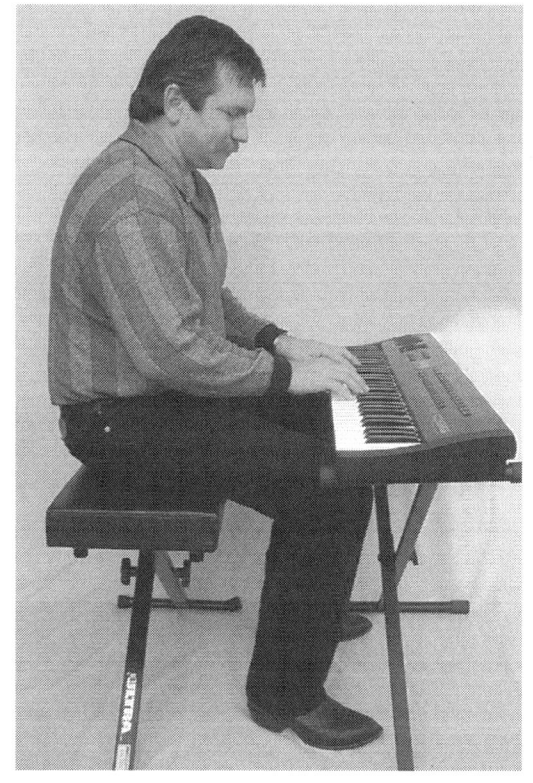

Proper sitting position

HAND POSITION

Your fingers should never be straight - but curved - like you are holding a grapefruit.

Correct Hand Position
(fingers curved)

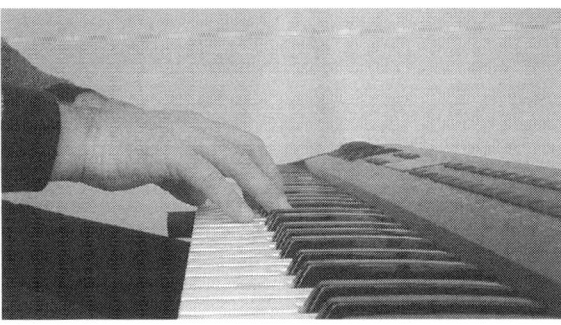

Incorrect Hand Position
(fingers straight)

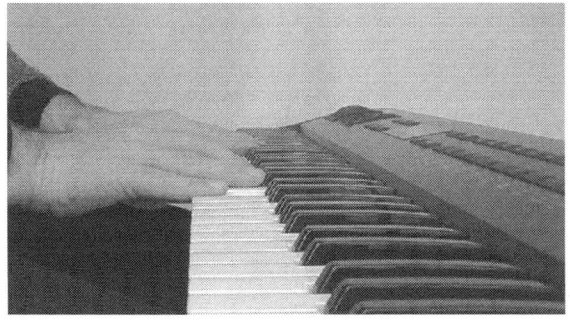

Use only the tips of your fingers to strike the keys.

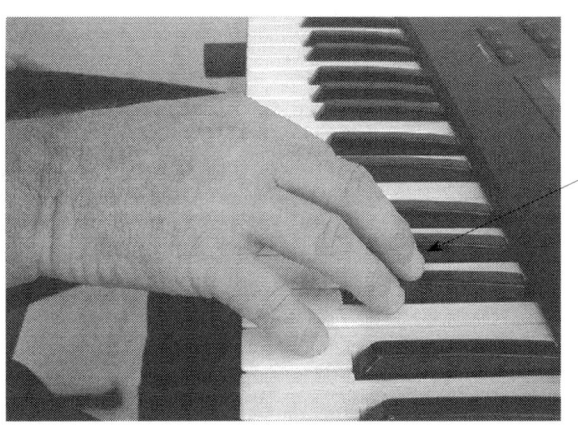

Tips of fingers on keys

LEARNING THE KEYS

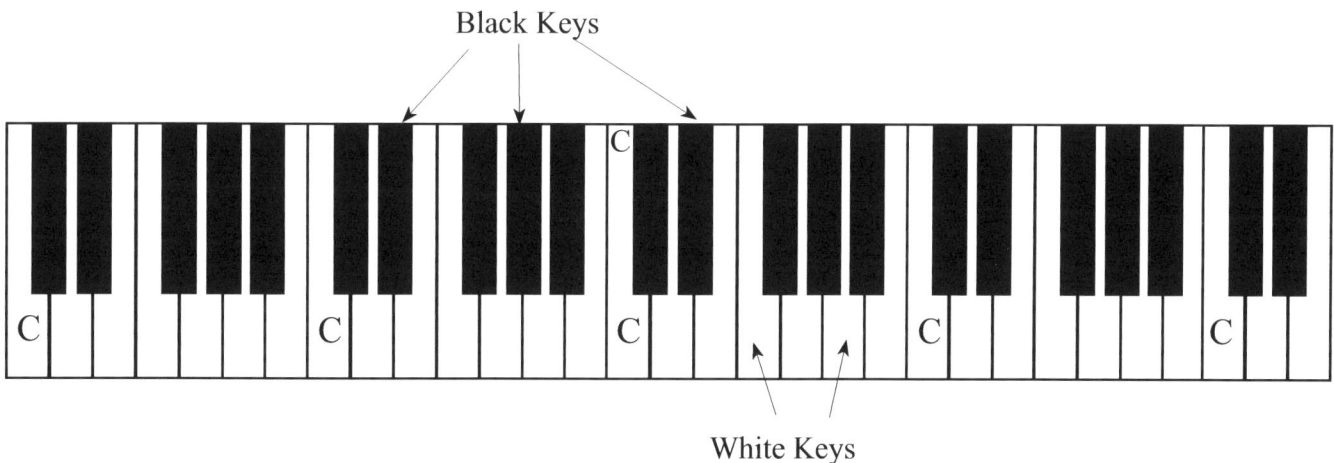

Pianos have 88 keys. Electronic keyboards usually have less. You may have 76, 61 or fewer.

The keys are divided into black and white keys. Black keys are divided into groups of twos and threes. The most important key for locating your place on the keyboard is middle C. The note C is always located directly left of the group of 2 black keys. Middle C is the C closest to the center of the keyboard.

EXERCISE 1

Find middle C and play it using any finger. Check your note by listening to the Video.

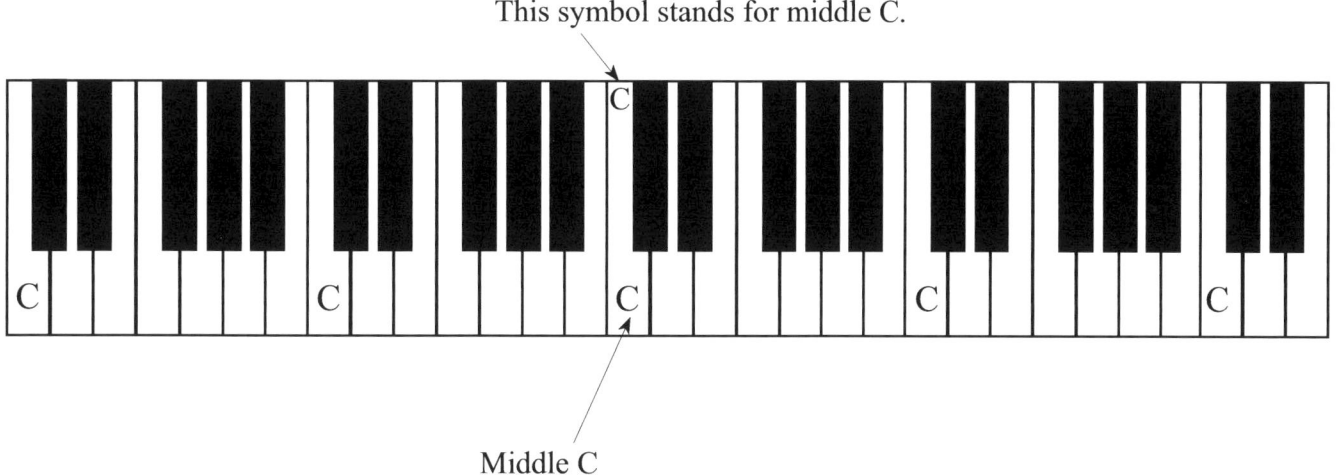

THE WHITE KEYS

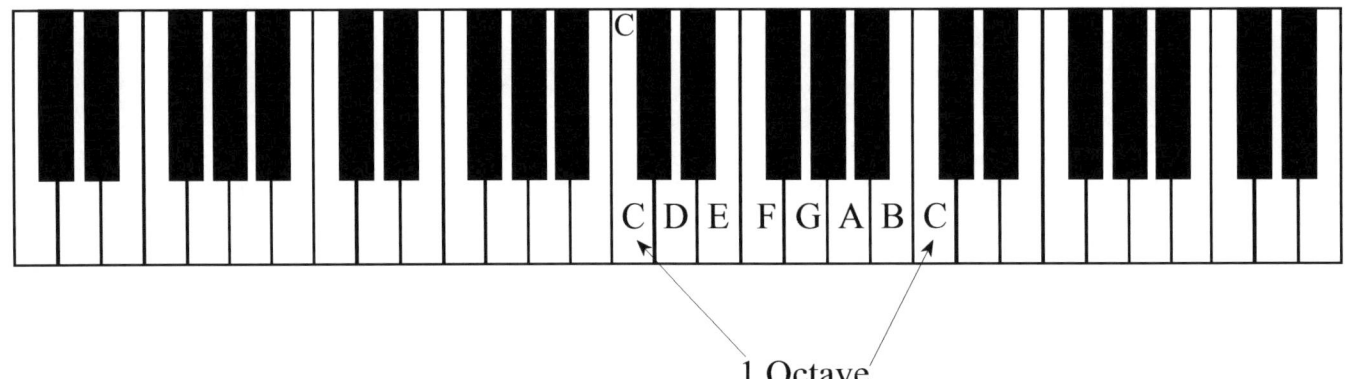

Starting with middle C, the white keys are:

C-D-E-F-G-A-B-C

Once you reach C again, it is an octave higher. An octave is a group of 8 notes from one C to the next C. The notes are named in this manner up and down the keyboard. Up the keyboard is to the right. Down the keyboard is to the left.

EXERCISE 2

Starting with middle C, memorize all the white keys up and down the keyboard.

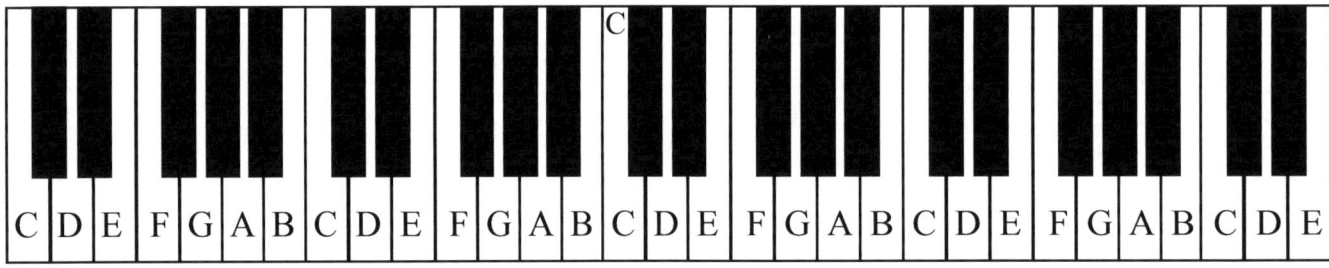

THE BLACK KEYS

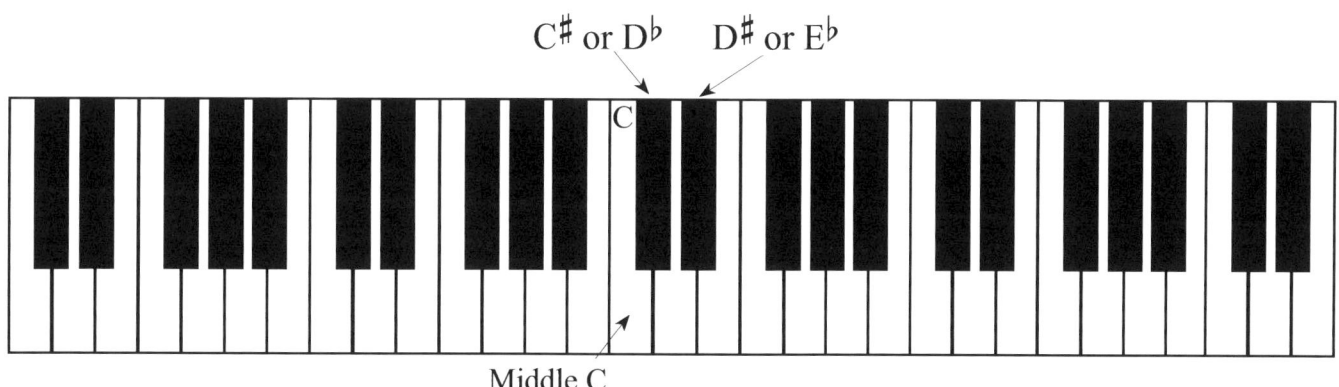

Notice that the black keys are grouped in twos and threes all the way up and down the keyboard. Find middle C again. Just to the right of middle C is the black key C sharp. Sharp means one key higher than the original note. This same black key could also be called D flat. Flat means one key lower than the original note. The black keys to the right of middle C are C sharp or D flat, D sharp or E flat.

♯ Symbol means sharp, or 1 key to the right
♭ Symbol means flat, or 1 key to the left

The group of three black keys are as follows: F sharp or G flat, G sharp or A flat, A sharp or B flat. Remember, each black key has two names, one using a sharp and the other a flat. Sharp means one key or half step higher than the white key to the left. Flat means one key or half step lower than the white key to the right.

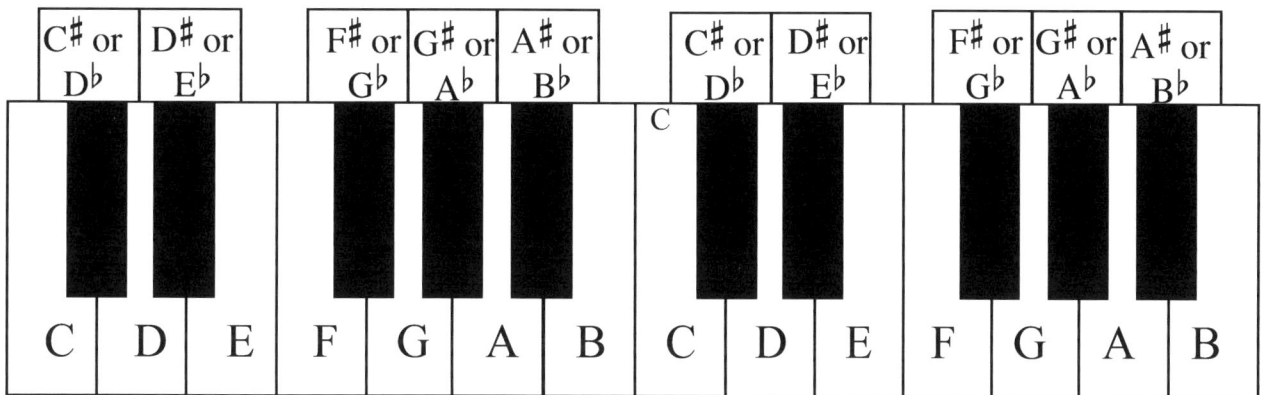

NUMBERING THE FINGERS

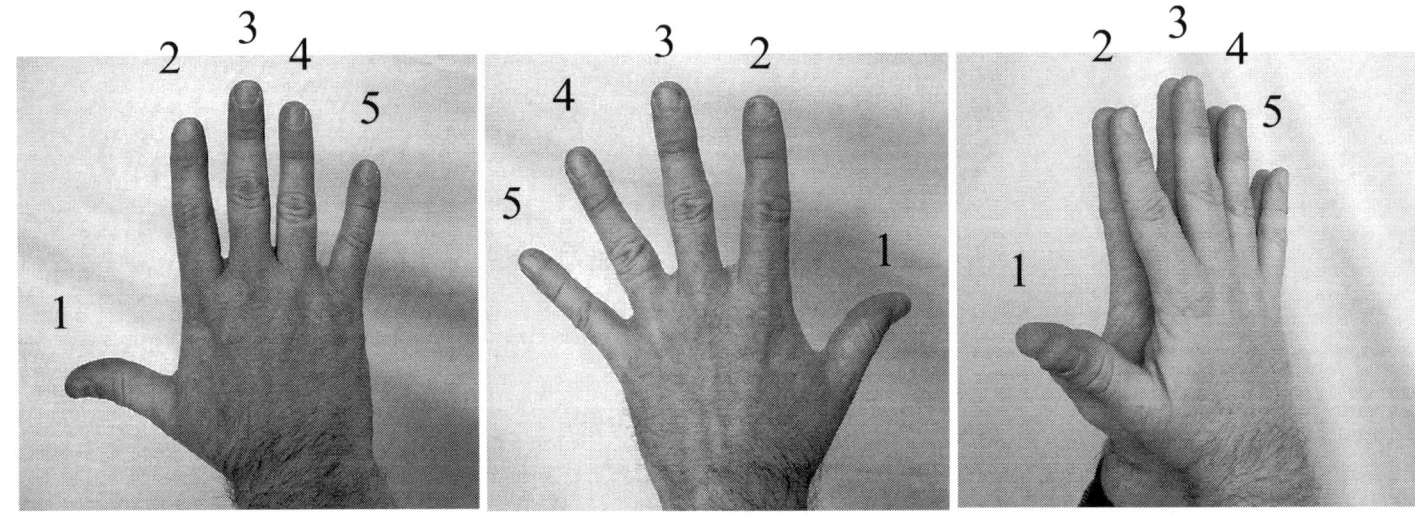

Right Hand **Left Hand** **Both Hands**

A BEGINNING EXERCISE

Here is a beginning song that doesn't require note reading. Use the Video to help you play this exercise.

EXERCISE 3

Find middle C and then place your right thumb on it. Now play middle C and the 4 white keys to the right or up the keyboard one at a time. Use your 1st finger, 2nd finger, 3rd finger, 4th finger, and 5th finger.

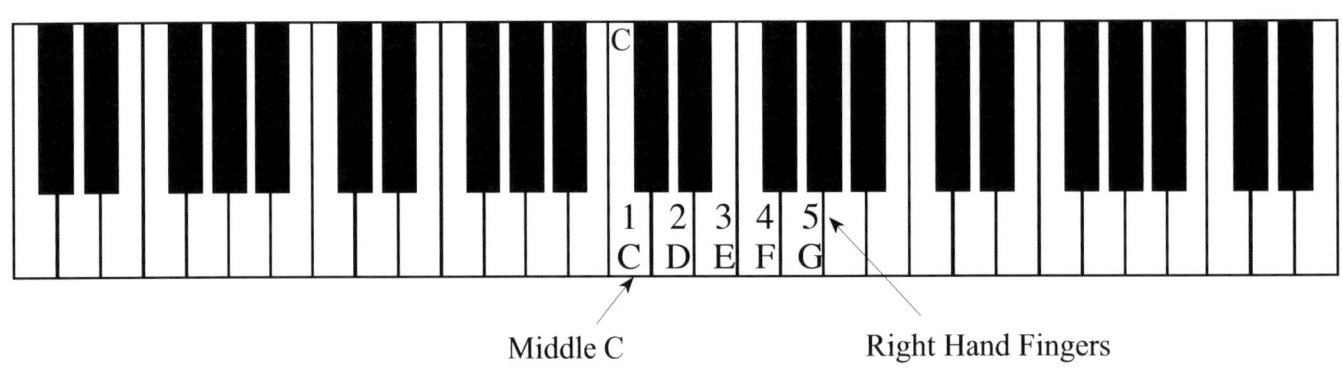

Middle C   Right Hand Fingers

8

EXERCISE 4

Start with your pinky on the note G (4 white keys to the right of middle C) and play this same exercise backwards or down the keyboard.

EXERCISE 5

Play Exercise 3 & 4 up (to the right) and down (to the left) the keyboard. Start with the thumb on your right hand. Practice this exercise until you can play it smoothly.

LEFT HAND EXERCISE

EXERCISE 6

Now let's play a similar exercise for the left hand. Place your left thumb on middle C and play the 4 white keys to the left, one at a time. Use your 1st finger, 2nd finger, 3rd finger, 4th finger, and 5th finger. Start with your left thumb and play this exercise down the keyboard. Begin with the note C.

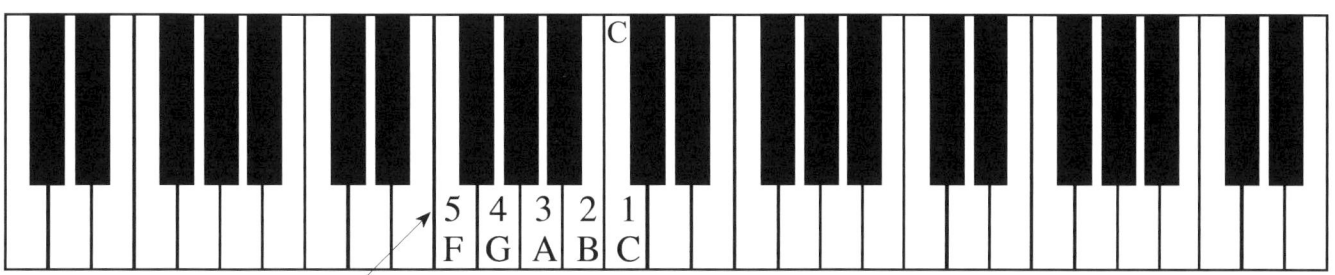

Left Hand Fingers

EXERCISE 7

Start with your pinky on the F note and play the exercise up the keyboard.

EXERCISE 8

Play Exercise 6 & 7 in both directions, starting with the thumb on your left hand. Begin with middle C.

THE QUARTER EXERCISE

Now play Exercise 9, but this time with a quarter balancing on the middle of your hand. Your goal is to keep the quarter balanced on the hand, not allowing it to fall off. This exercise will promote good hand position, and keep your arms and wrists from moving too much. This proper hand technique will take some practice, so be patient.

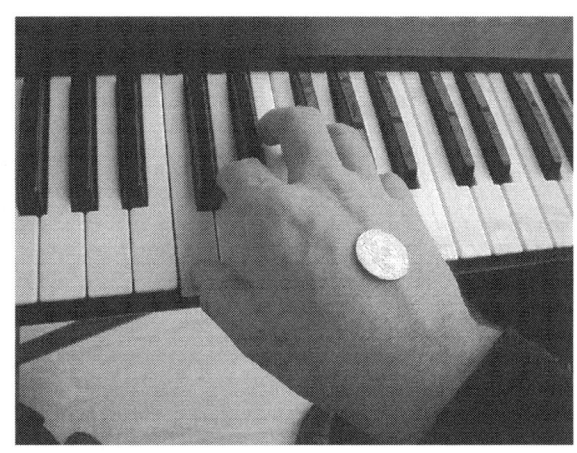

EXERCISE 9

Practice Exercises 5 and 8 up and down the keyboard with a quarter balanced on the top of your hand. First do the right hand and then the left.

This is a good beginning exercise to develop finger dexterity and become familiar with the keyboard. Make this exercise a regular part of your practice, and try to practice every day for 30 minutes or more.

REVIEW

Practice what you have learned until you are comfortable playing these exercises. At this point you should know:

1. How to set up your keyboard, be able to turn it on, and adjust the volume.
2. Proper playing position. Sit up straight, don't slouch, and have your fingers, arms, and hands in the correct position.
3. Understand the keys on the keyboard and be able to find middle C.
4. Know the correct finger numbers for the right and left hand.

SECTION 2
RHYTHM & NOTES

For Audio & Video Access, go to this internet address:
http://cvls.com/extras/keyboard/

RIGHT HAND ETUDE

You can now use what we have learned so far to play a song.

EXERCISE 10

Using the diagram below and the Video to help you, play these notes with your right hand:

C-D-C-F-C-D-E-D-C

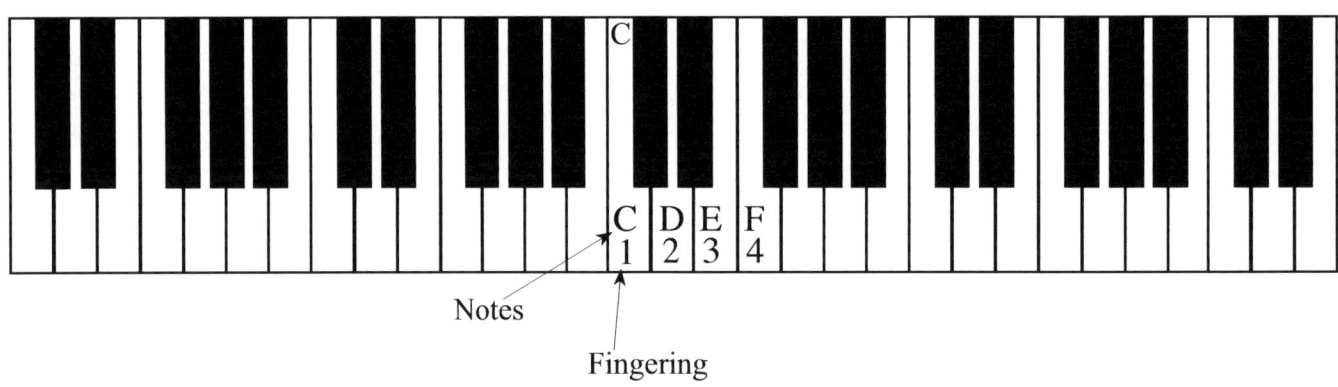

EXERCISE 11

Play the same notes, but this time make each note last 4 counts. Count 1 2 3 4 for each note. Count along with the Video.

C-D-C-F-C-D-E-D-C

EXERCISE 12

Play Exercise 11 once more, but this time with the band accompanying you. You will hear a 4 beat count off from the drums telling you when to start.

LEFT HAND REGGAE

We will now play a similar song for the left hand.

EXERCISE 13

Use the diagram below and the Video to help you play these notes with your left hand:

C-B-C-G-C-B-A-B-C

EXERCISE 14

Play the same notes as Exercise 13, but this time make each note last 4 counts.

EXERCISE 15

Play it once more, but this time with the band. You will here a 4 beat count off from the drums telling you when to start.

PRACTICE TIPS

1. Practice slowly at first. Let your brain and fingers get used to doing what you want them to do.
2. Repetition is the key to learning music. Practice exercises over and over until they are comfortable. It is important that you repeat things correctly.
3. Find the most difficult section in a song or exercise, and practice it most. Just playing through the whole song over and over will slow your progress.

THE TREBLE CLEF

The Musical Alphabet consists of just 7 letters:

A-B-C-D-E-F-G

To read music we must be able to find these notes on the staff. The staff is a system of 5 lines and 4 spaces telling you which notes to play. The symbol to the left is called the Clef. We'll start with the Treble Clef. It tells you what each line and space means, kind of like the key to a map.

When music is written in the treble clef, the 5 lines represent these notes:

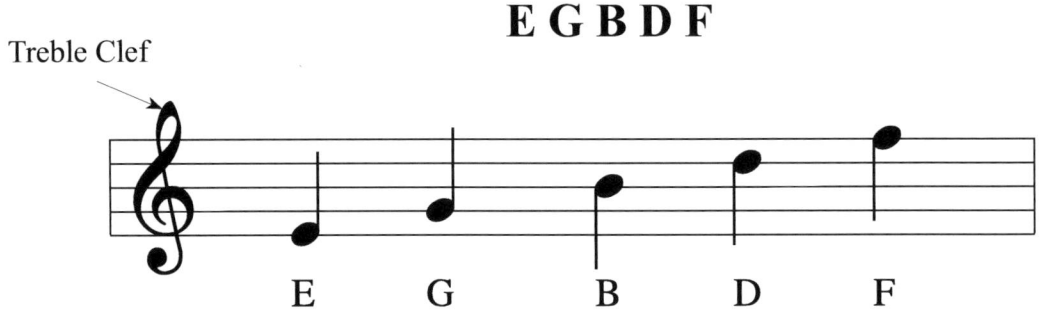

You can remember this by the phrase *Every Good Boy Does Fine*.

The spaces represent the letters:

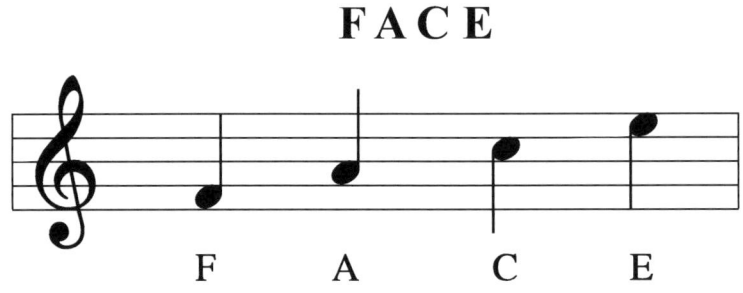

Remember the word FACE. You should memorize these notes and their location on the staff.

The staff is divided into sections that are called measures. The lines are called bar lines.

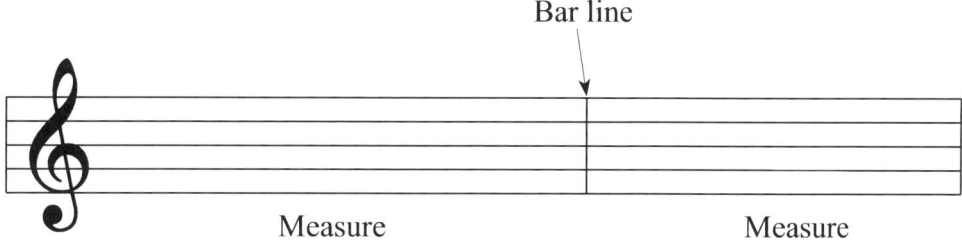

TIME SIGNATURE

Each measure gets a certain number of counts. We will start with each measure getting 4 counts or beats. Count (1 2 3 4, 1 2 3 4). This is called the time signature and tells us how many beats are in a measure. 4/4 means there are 4 beats to a measure. If it were 3/4, it would mean there are 3 beats to a measure.

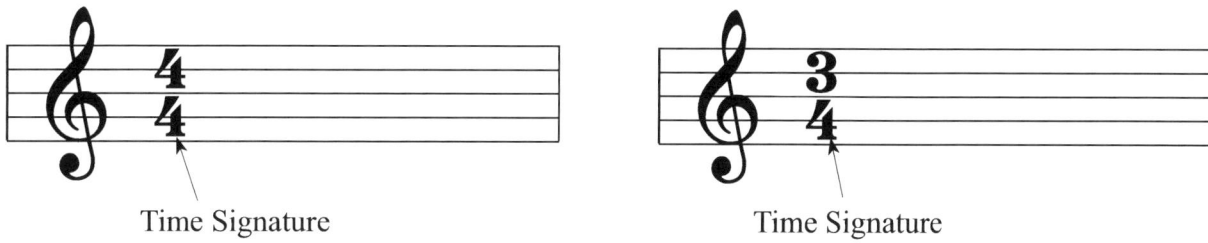

NOTES

There are several parts that make up a note: the head, the stem, and with some notes, the flag.

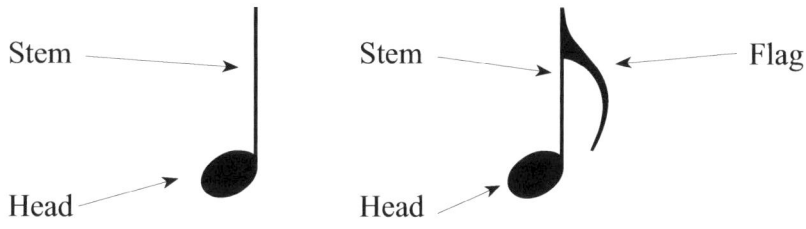

15

NOTE VALUES

Start by learning 3 types of notes, the whole note which lasts 4 beats, the half note which lasts 2 beats, and the quarter note which lasts 1 beat.

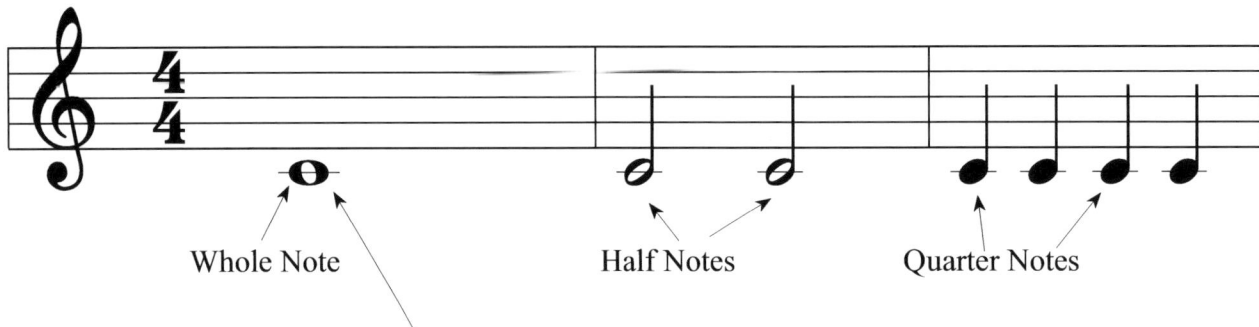

This is where middle C is written on the staff. The line below the staff is called a ledger line, and it allows notes to be written below (and above) the staff.

RESTS

Rests are another type of notation you must learn. Rests tell you how many beats <u>not</u> to play. The names of rests correspond to the names of notes. For example, the whole note rest, like the whole note, gets 4 beats.

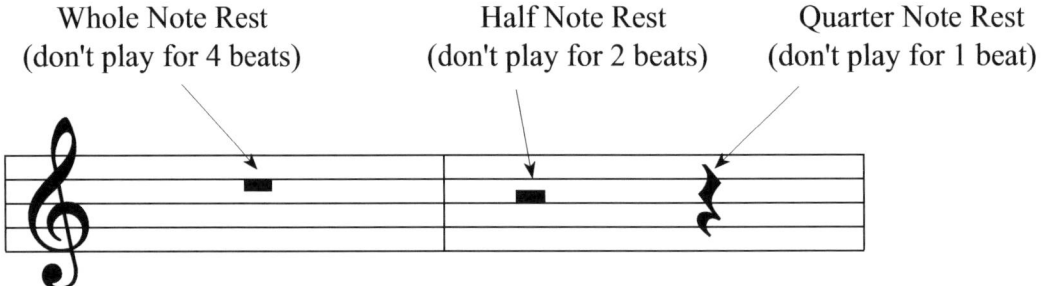

EXERCISE 16

Play middle C, first as a whole note, then as two half notes, and finally as four quarter notes. Refer to the notation above.

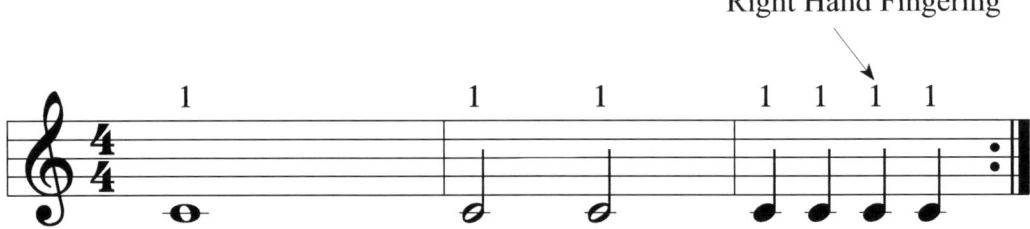

MORE NOTES

Here are the D, E, F, and G notes and their location on the keyboard relative to middle C.

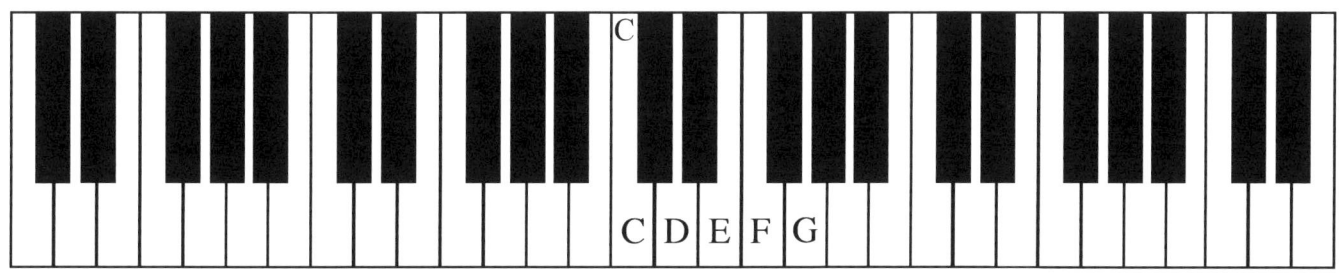

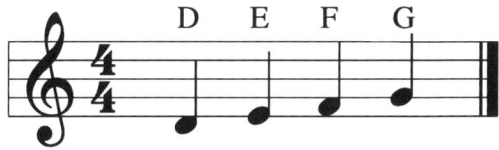

Take some time to memorize these notes, as we will be using them in the next exercise.

EXERCISE 17

Play this exercise using the C, D, E, F, & G notes.

Right Hand Fingering

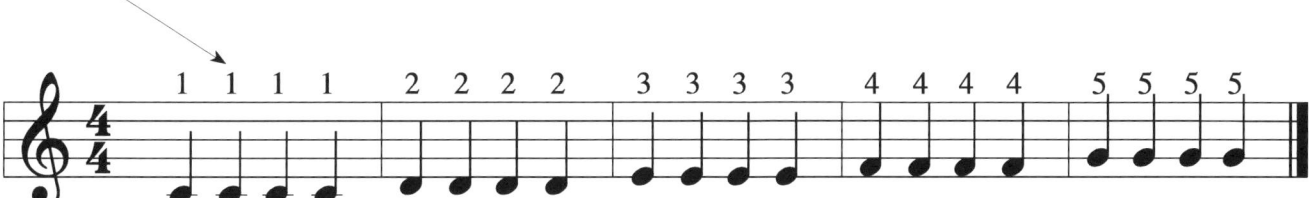

SONG FOR RIGHT HAND

We can now play the exercise we learned on page 9 using the right hand, but this time reading notes. Start with the right thumb on middle C. Practice slowly at first, then speed it up and play along with the band on the Video. Refer to the finger numbers above the notes. There will be a four beat count off from the drums. Note the repeat sign, which means to repeat the entire exercise.

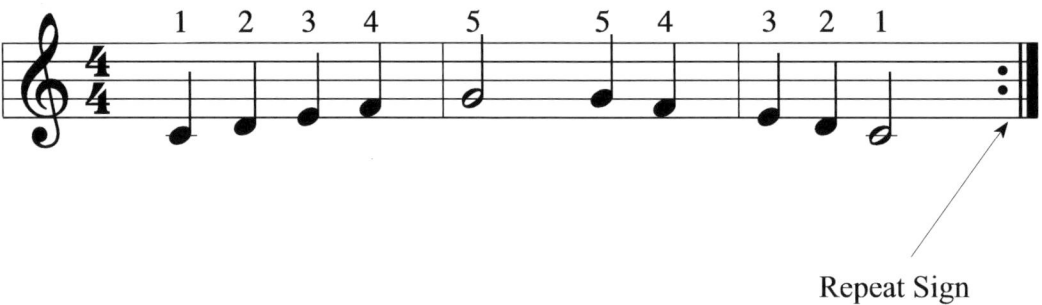

Repeat Sign

CLAIR DE LUNE

Here is a simple song using the treble clef. Watch the notation and play along at a reduced speed. Once you are comfortable with all the notes and fingerings, speed it up and play along with the band.

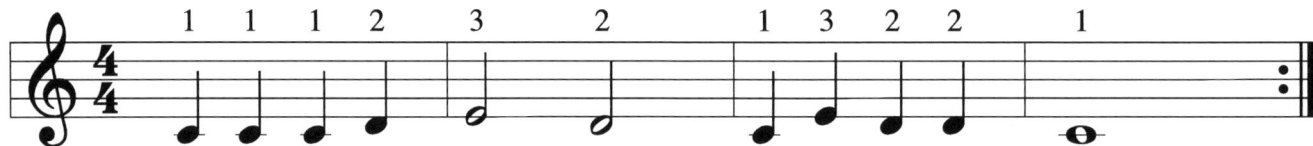

ODE TO JOY

Here is a slightly longer song using the notes you've learned. Practice first with the Video at a slow tempo, then speed it up and play along with the band.

SIMPLE MELODY

Notice these logos. This indicates bonus songs in the book that are not on the Video. Make sure you practice these songs along with the audio tracks.

19

MARY HAD A LITTLE LAMB

RIGHT AHEAD

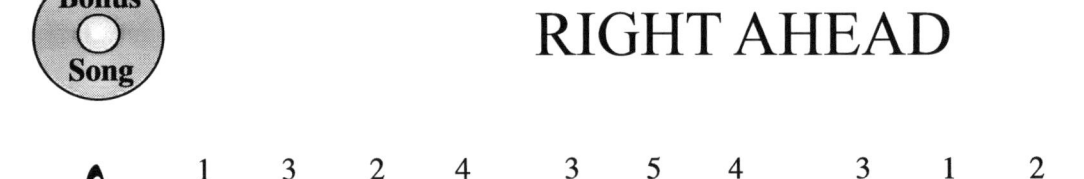

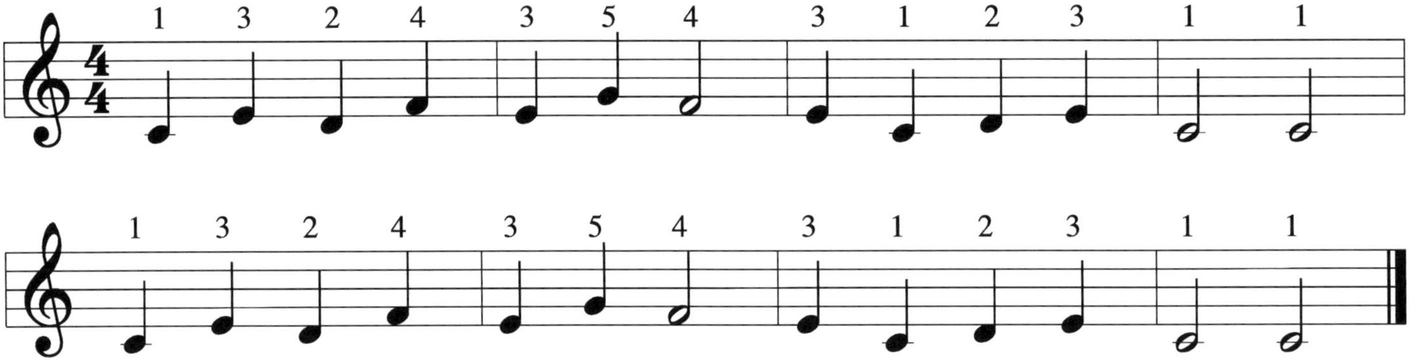

FINGER EASE

THE BASS CLEF

The piano uses two clefs. We have already learned the Treble Clef, and now we will learn the Bass Clef. Generally, the right hand will play the treble clef and the left hand will play the bass clef.

The lines in the bass clef represent the notes G B D F and A. Think *Good Birds Don't Fly Away.*

Bass Clef

The spaces represent A C E and G. Think *All Cows Eat Grass.*

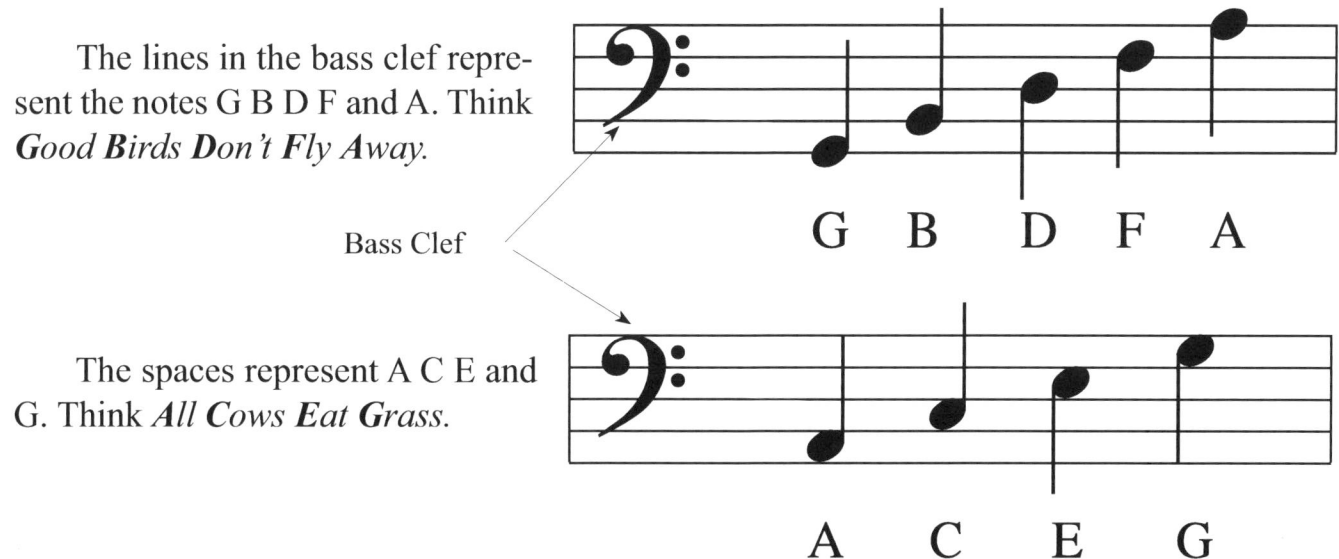

NOTES IN THE BASS CLEF

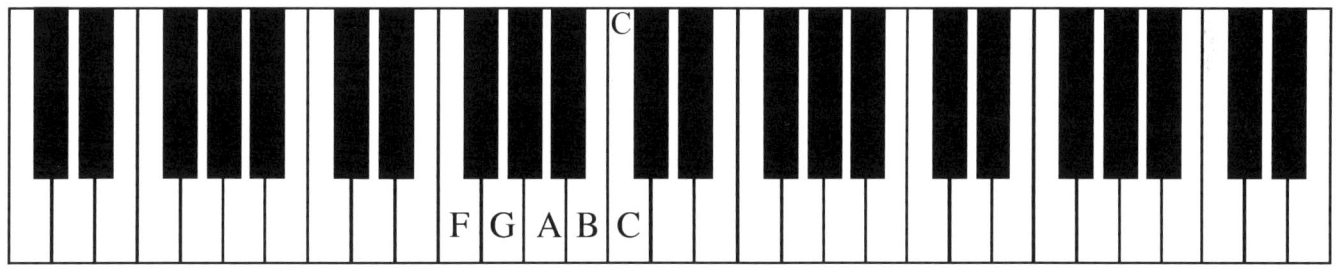

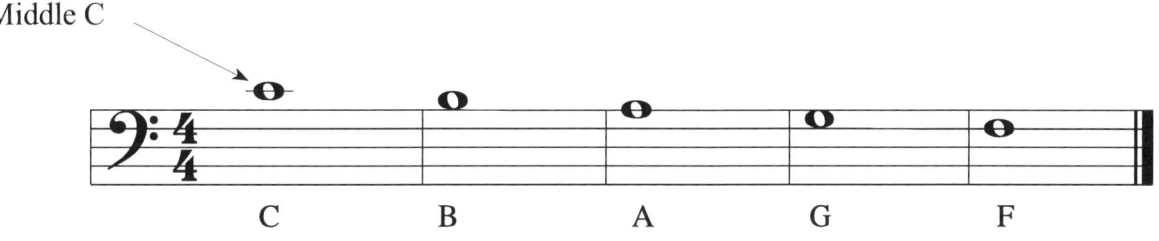

Memorize these 5 notes in the Bass Clef.

21

EXERCISE 18

Play this exercise using the notes you have learned in the bass clef. Notice that each note is a quarter note.

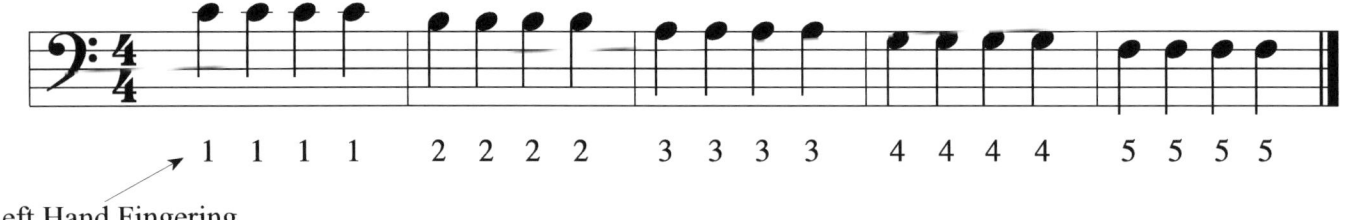

Left Hand Fingering

SONG FOR THE LEFT HAND

Now play the exercise for the left hand on page 10, but this time using the bass clef. Start with your left thumb on middle C. Practice slowly at first, then speed it up and play along with the band on Video.

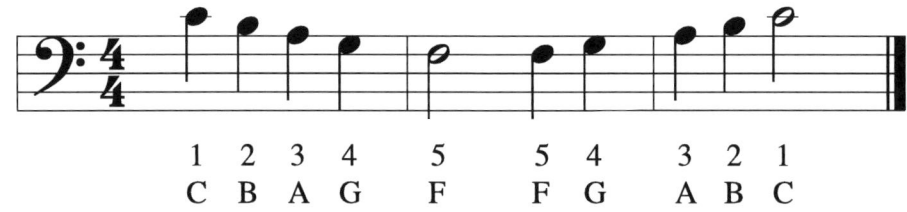

MORE NOTES IN THE BASS CLEF

To learn the next song, you must first learn some lower notes in the bass clef.

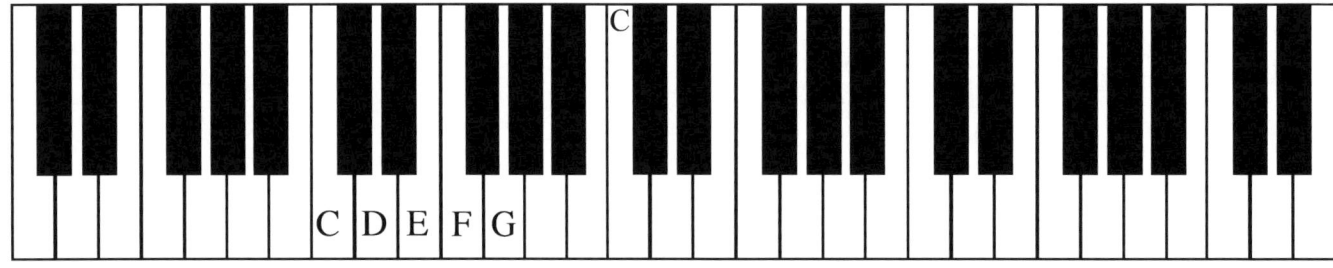

Take time to memorize these notes.

22

EXERCISE 19

Starting with the left pinky on C (one octave below middle C), practice this exercise.

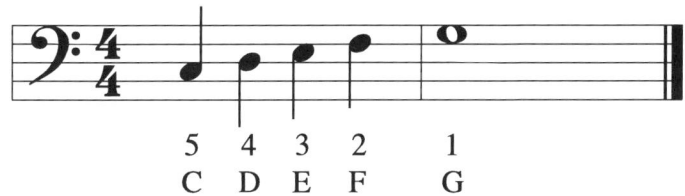

```
5  4  3  2    1
C  D  E  F    G
```

EXERCISE 20

Now start with your left thumb, playing the same exercise down the keyboard.

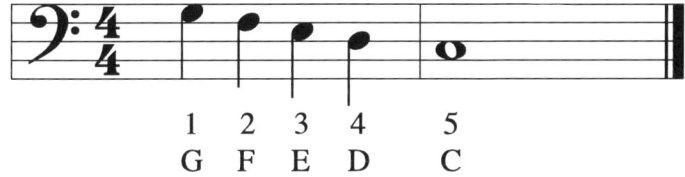

```
1  2  3  4    5
G  F  E  D    C
```

CLAIR DE LUNE BASS CLEF

Use the extra notes you have just learned to play *Clair De Lune* in the Bass Clef. Practice slowly at first, then play along with the band on the Video.

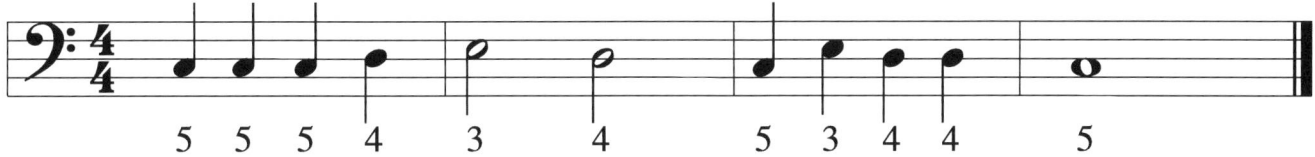

```
5  5  5  4    3     4     5  3  4  4    5
```

23

STEPS

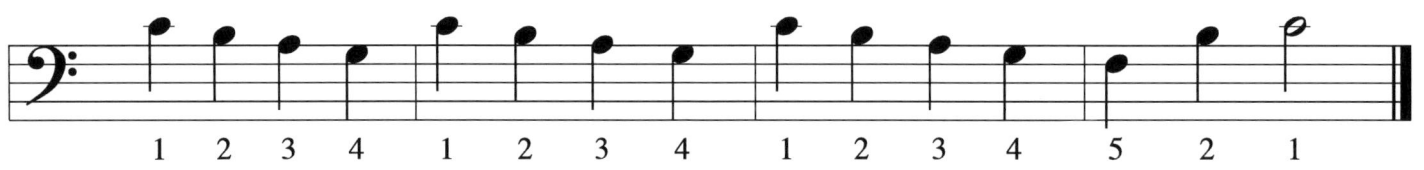

BASS CLEF STUDY

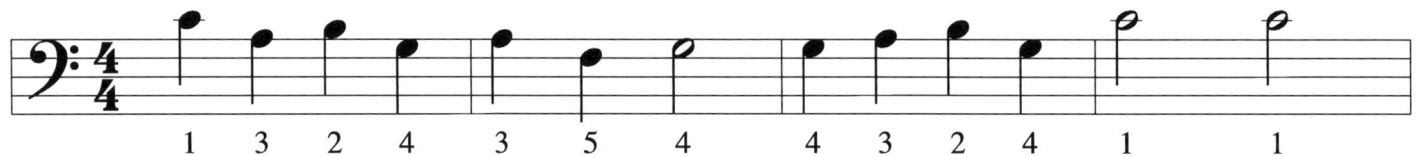
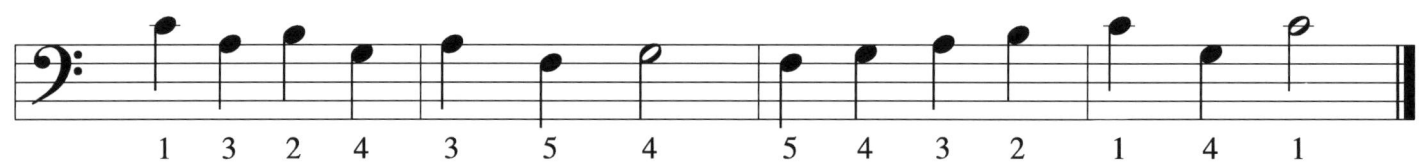

Notice these logos. This indicates bonus songs in the book that are not on the Video. Make sure you practice these songs along with the audio tracks.

24

THE GRAND STAFF

We will now combine both the Treble Clef and the Bass Clef to make the Grand Staff. Middle C is located between the two staffs. It may be useful to practice each clef individually, then read both at the same time. Remember to read the notes, not just the fingerings.

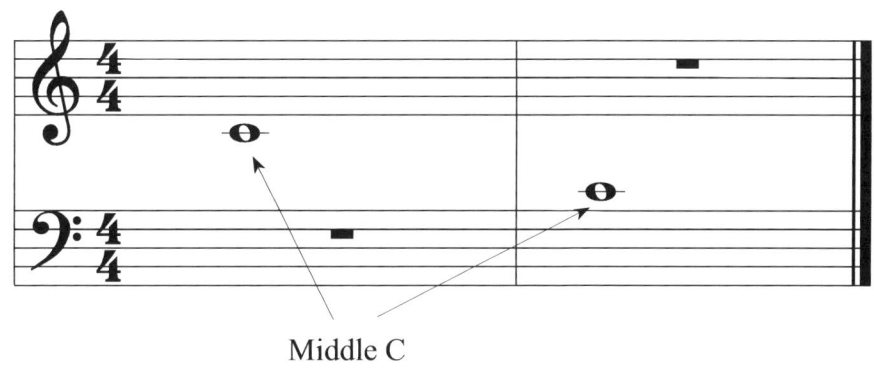

Middle C

GRAND STAFF SONG 1

Practice this exercise slowly at first, then play along with the band on the Video. Play through this exercise two times.

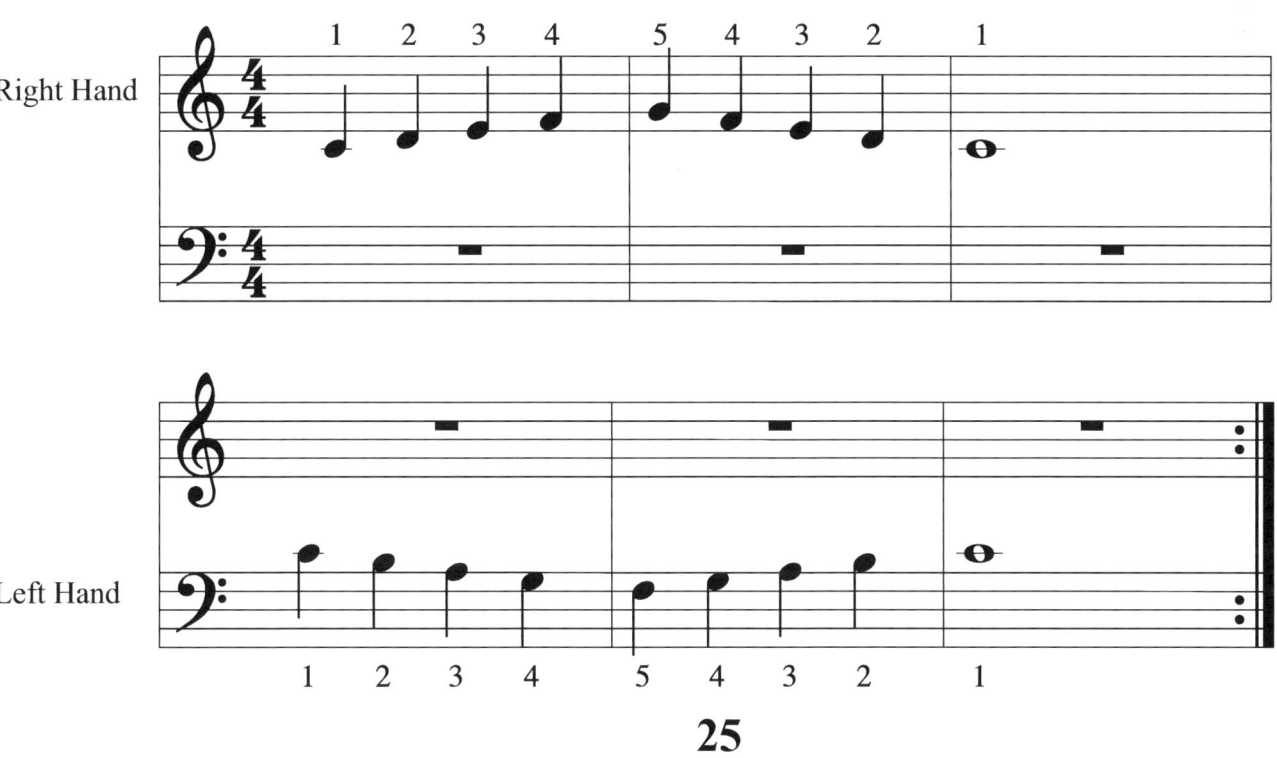

EXERCISE 21

Play this exercise using the right hand. Start with your thumb on middle C.

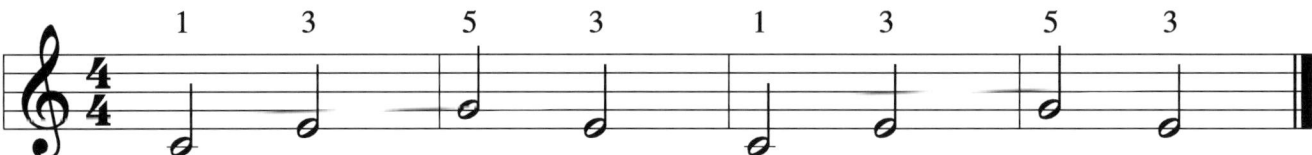

EXERCISE 22

Play this exercise using the left hand. Start with the thumb on middle C.

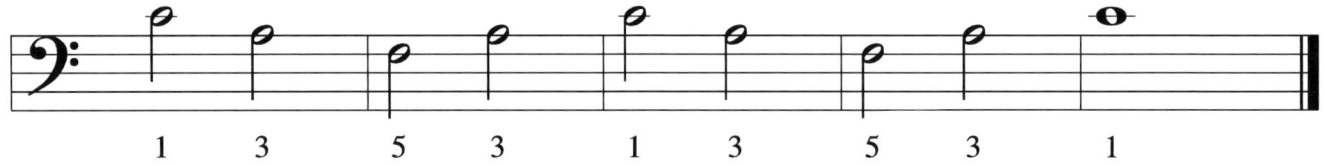

GRAND STAFF 2

Now combine both parts. Practice slowly and evenly until you are comfortable playing the entire song, then play along with the band on the Video.

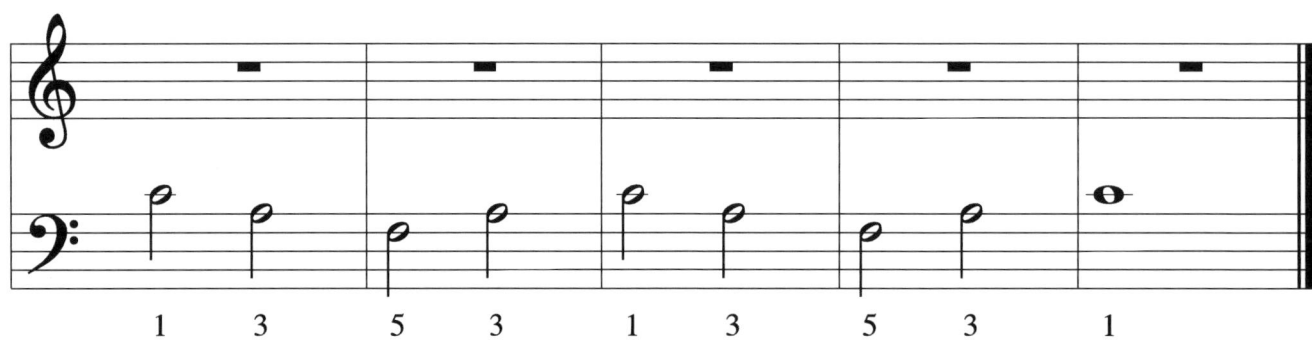

ODE TO JOY BASS LINE

Here is the left hand part (the bass line) to *Ode to Joy*. In the last measure, you must use a new technique where you will cross your thumb under your 3rd finger. Here is how it should look.

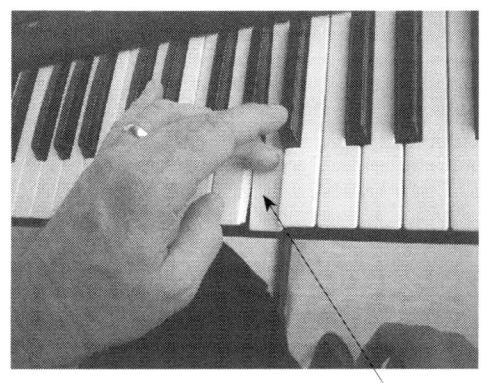

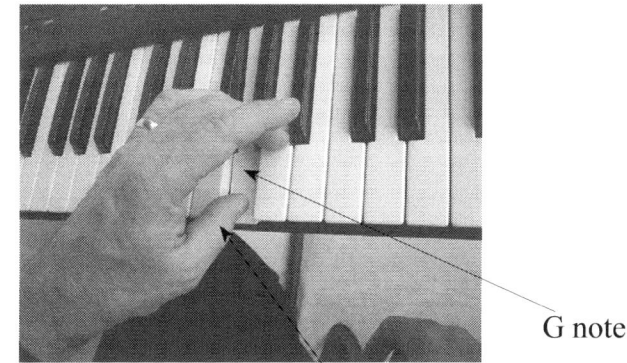

Starting position   A note

Thumb crossing under 3rd finger   G note

EXERCISE 23

Practice this cross-under technique.

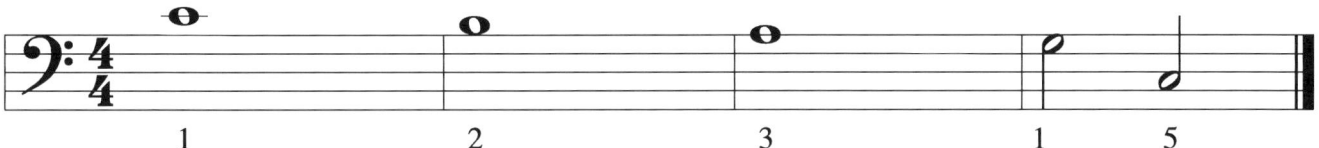

EXERCISE 24

Below is the bass line to *Ode to Joy*. Practice this bass line slowly and evenly. Pay particular attention to the cross under technique.

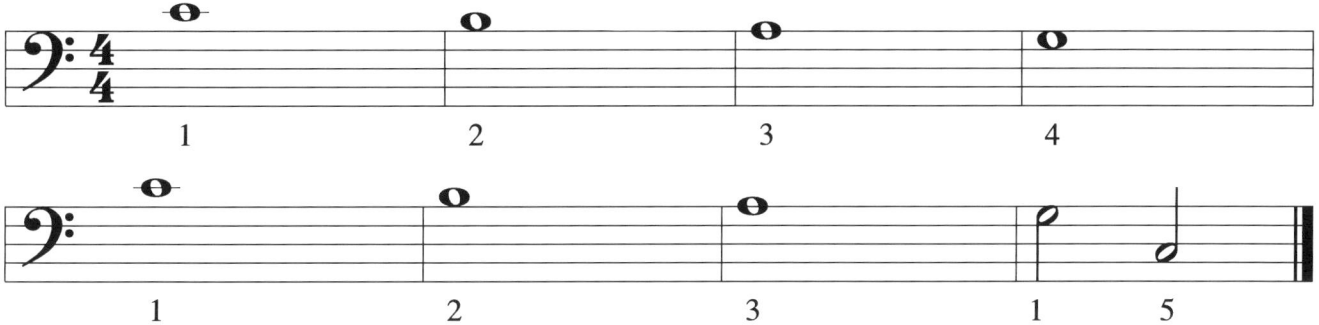

ODE TO JOY
GRAND STAFF

Now combine both parts and play *Ode to Joy*. Reading both clefs and playing both parts may be difficult at first, so be patient. Practice slowly until you can play the song smoothly, then play along with the band on the Video.

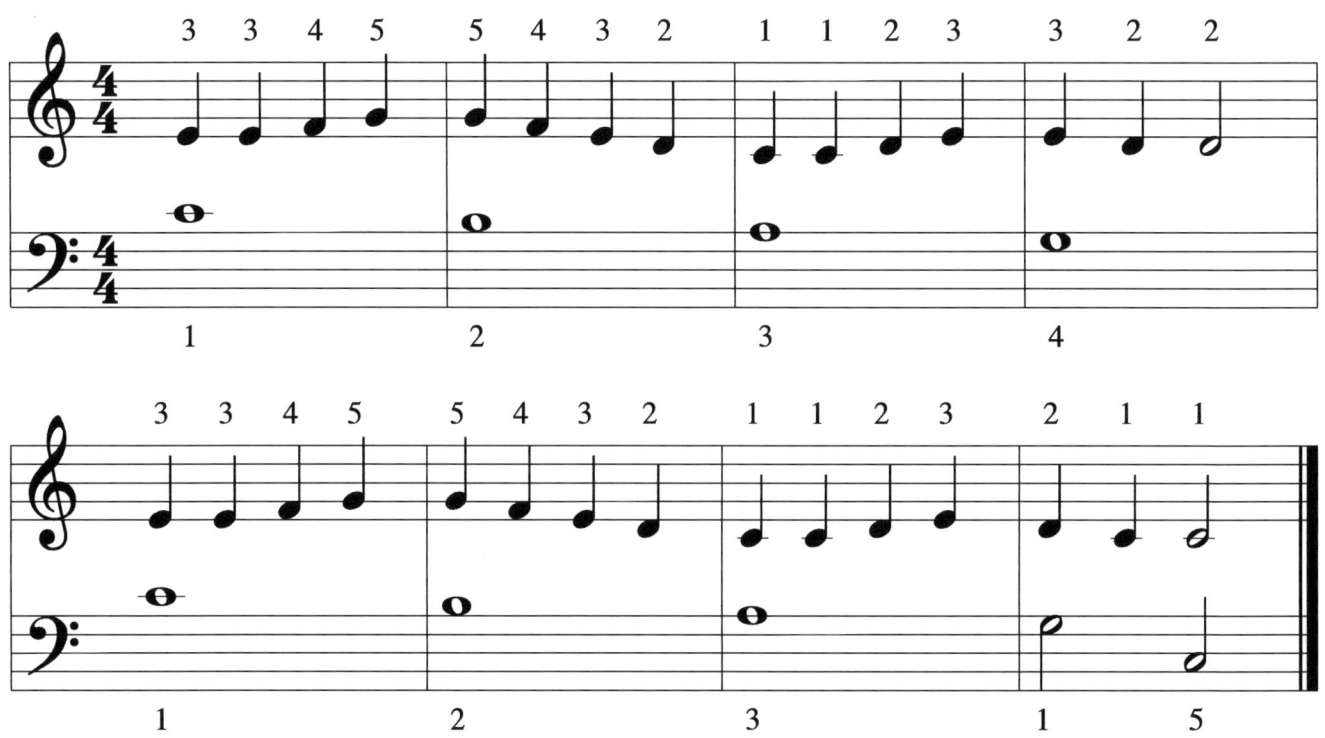

EXERCISE 25

Here is another song using the Grand Staff. Start with the right hand part.

EXERCISE 26

Now practice the left hand part.

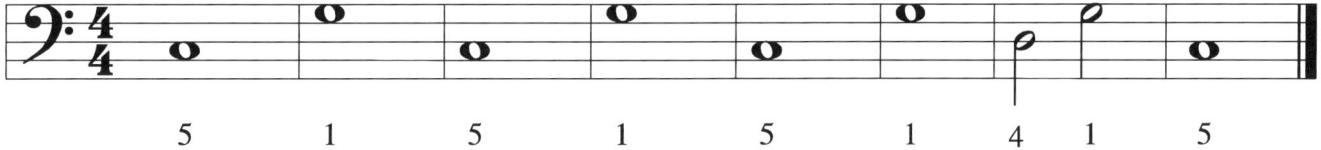

Now practice the whole song. We'll divide it into 2 parts. Practice slowly and evenly at first, then play it up to speed with the band.

MAJOR MELODY

29

SECTION 3
CHORDS

For Audio & Video Access, go to this internet address:
http://cvls.com/extras/keyboard/

CHORDS

In this section, we are going to play chords and we'll learn a few more notes in the treble clef. It may be helpful to remember the treble clef staff lines using the phrase *Every Good Boy Does Fine* and the spaces using *F A C E*. Review page 14.

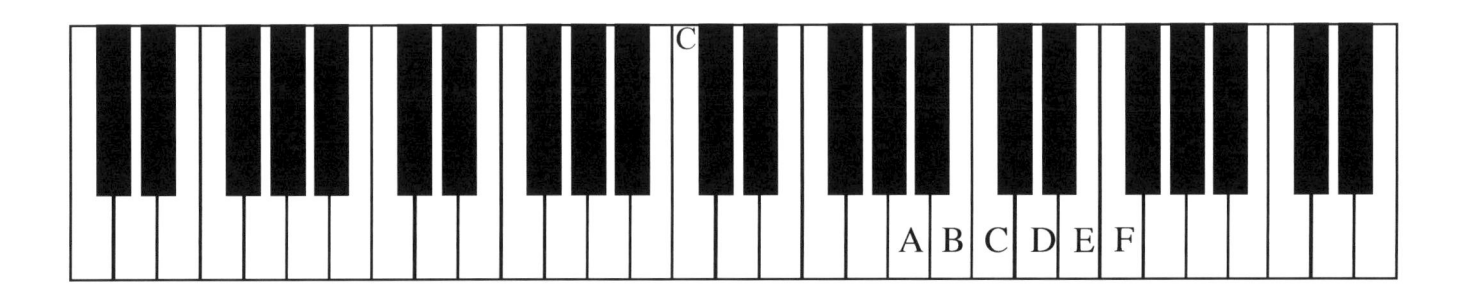

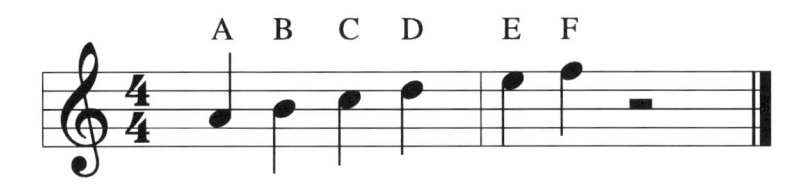

Take a few moments here and memorize the new notes in the diagram above. We will be referring to them in this section and throughout the rest of the course.

EXERCISE 27

Play all the notes you know in the treble clef. Start on the note middle C. For this example, use the index finger on your right hand to play all the notes.

We can now learn to play chords on the keyboard. Chords are constructed by playing 3 or more notes at the same time. Start with a C major chord.

EXERCISE 28

Play the notes C, E, and G at the same time with your right hand. Use your 1st finger, 3rd finger, and 5th finger.

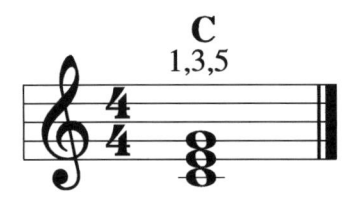

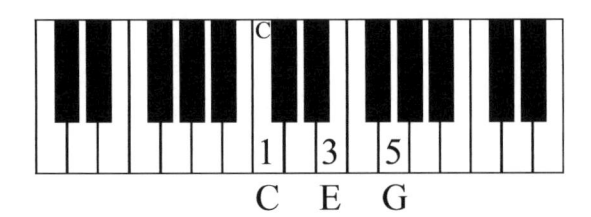

EXERCISE 29

Use your 1st, 3rd, and 5th fingers of the right hand to play chords all the way up the keyboard. Start on middle C.

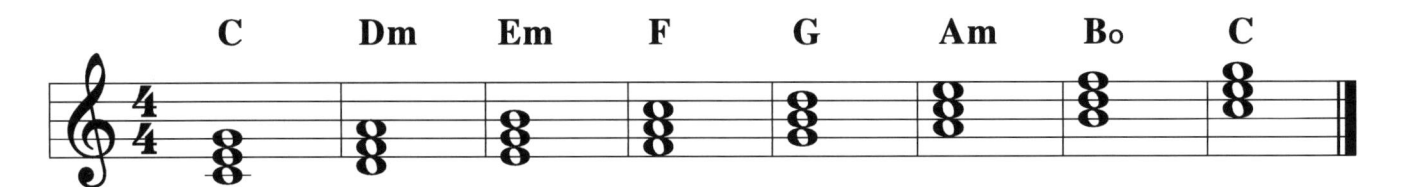

C   Dm   Em   F   G   Am   Bo   C

EXERCISE 30

Now do the same exercise with your left hand. Use your 1st, 3rd, and 5th fingers.

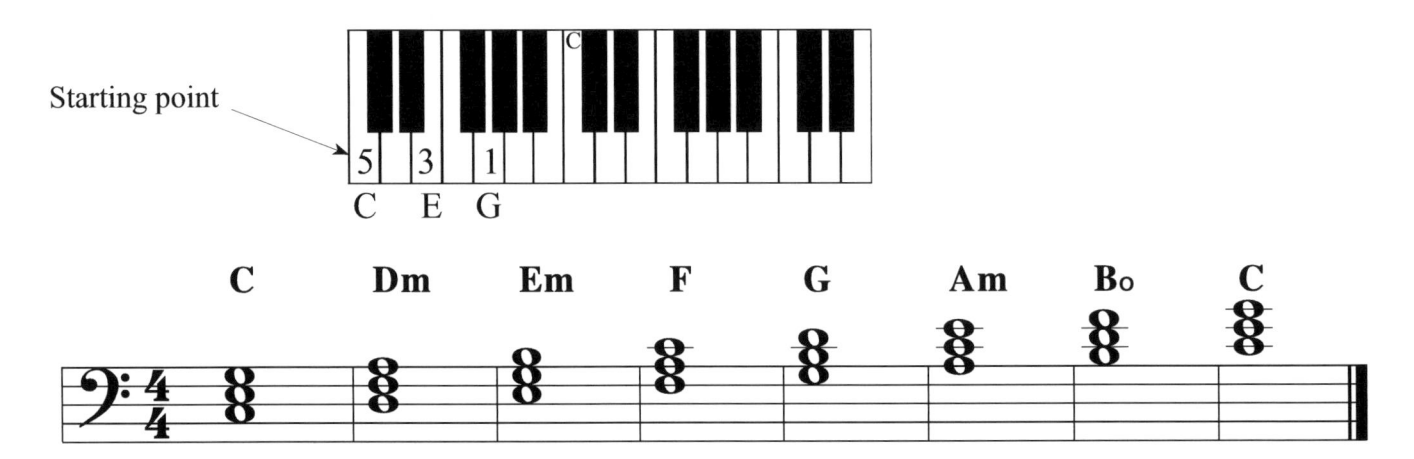

Starting point

C   E   G

C   Dm   Em   F   G   Am   Bo   C

EXERCISE 31

Now we'll use chords to play a song. Start by playing a C Major with the right hand.

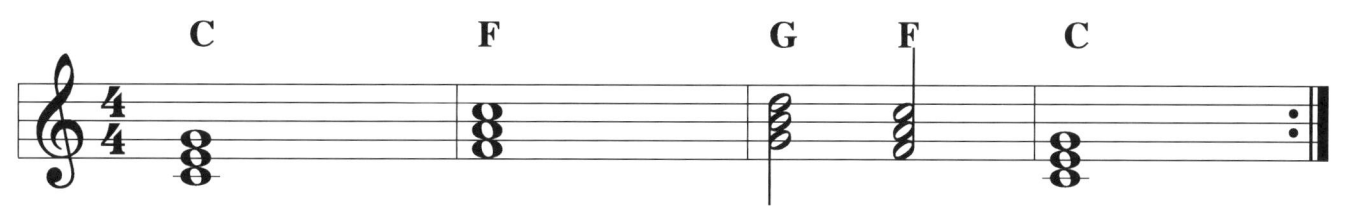

EXERCISE 32

Now use your left hand to play the same exercise.

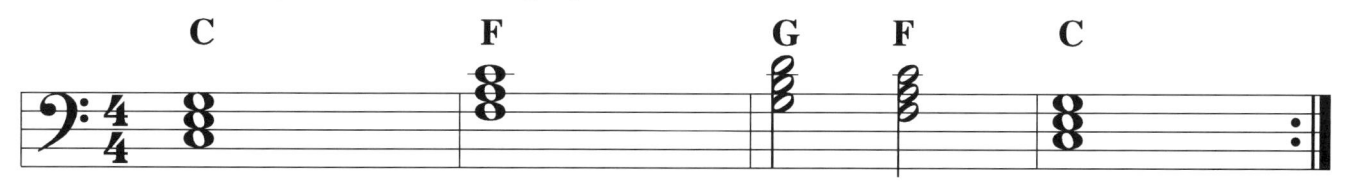

Let's try the whole song. Practice at a slow tempo first, then speed it up and play along with the band on the Video.

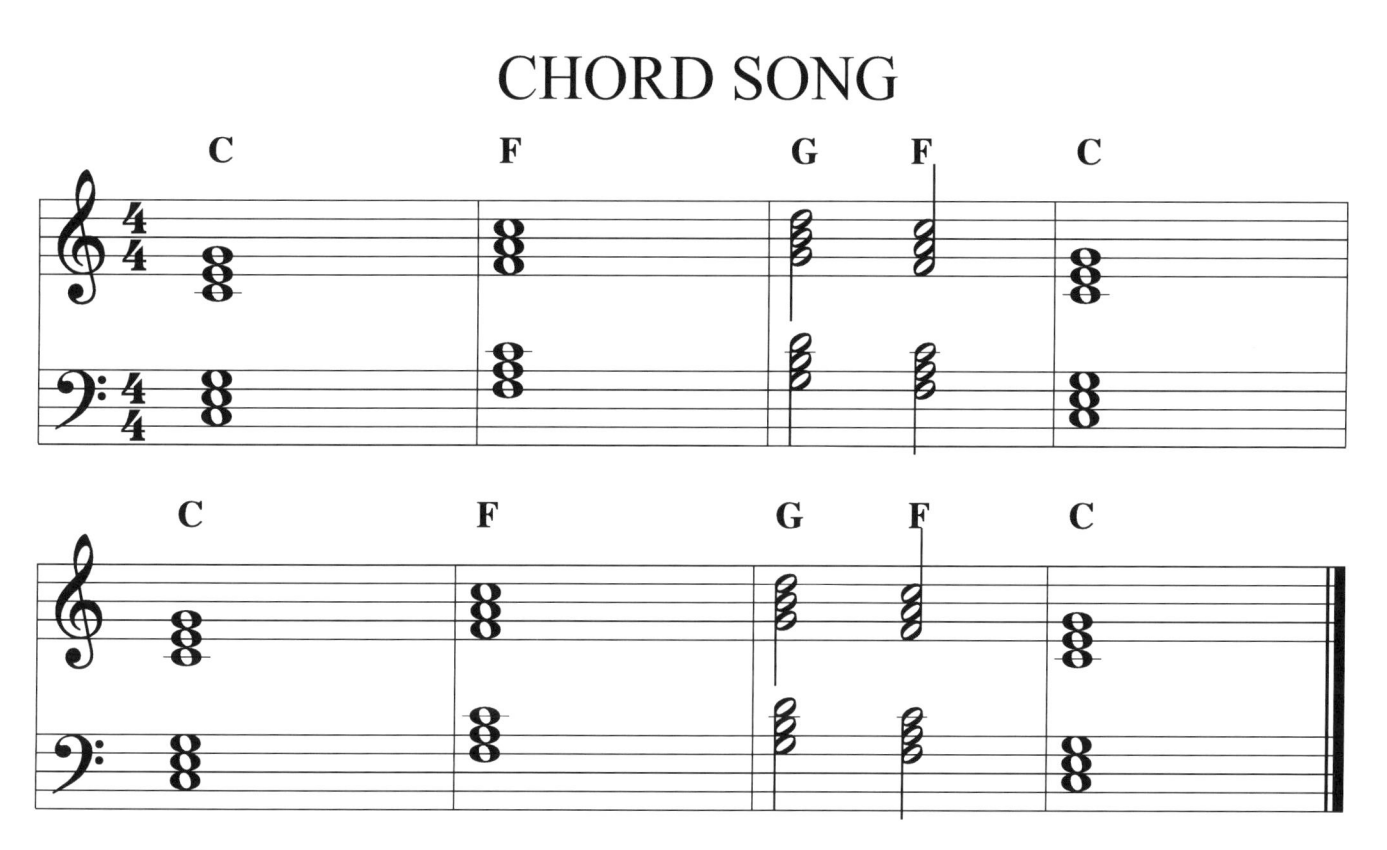

CHORD SONG

CHORD WORKOUT

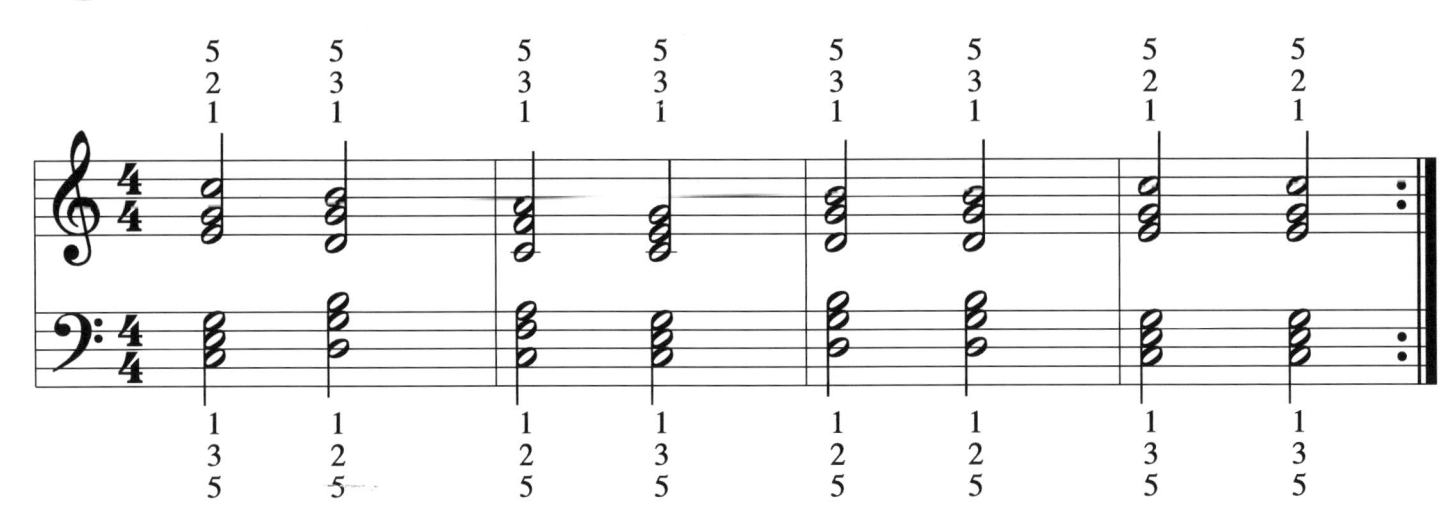

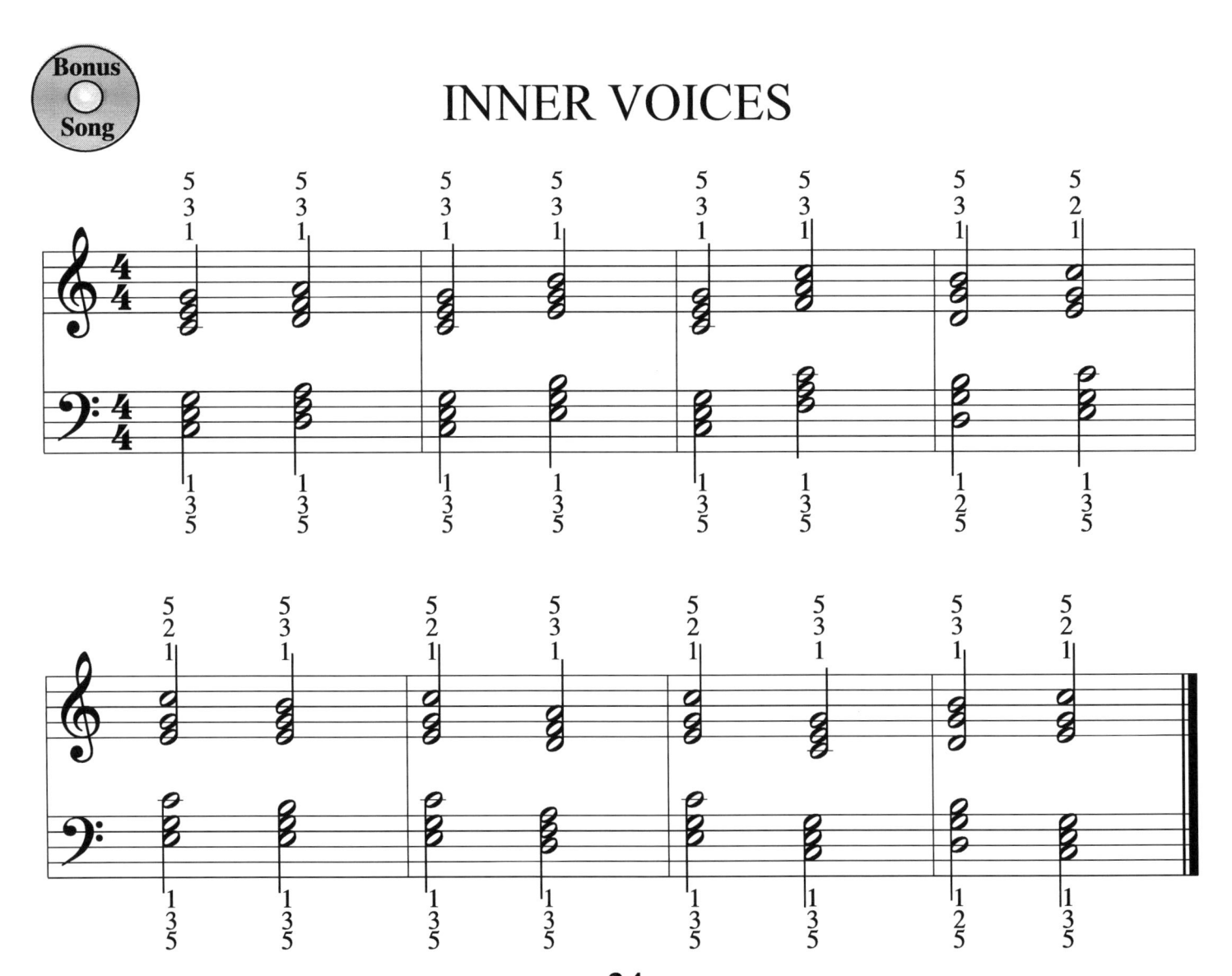

INNER VOICES

CHORDS WITH A BASS LINE

Now play the same tune you learned on page 33, but this time play chords with the right hand and the bass line with the left hand.

EXERCISE 33

Here are the notes we will play with the left hand. Practice this left hand part until you are very comfortable with it.

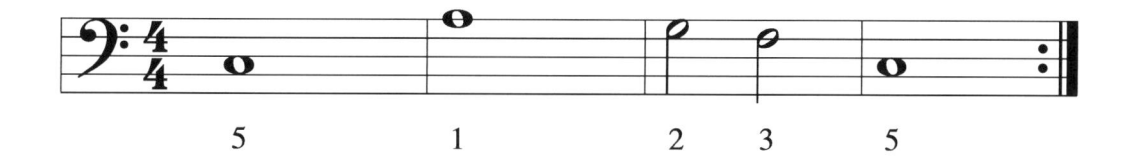

CHORD SONG/ BASS LINE

Now play both parts. Practice slowly at first. When you are comfortable with both hands, speed it up and play along with the band on the Video.

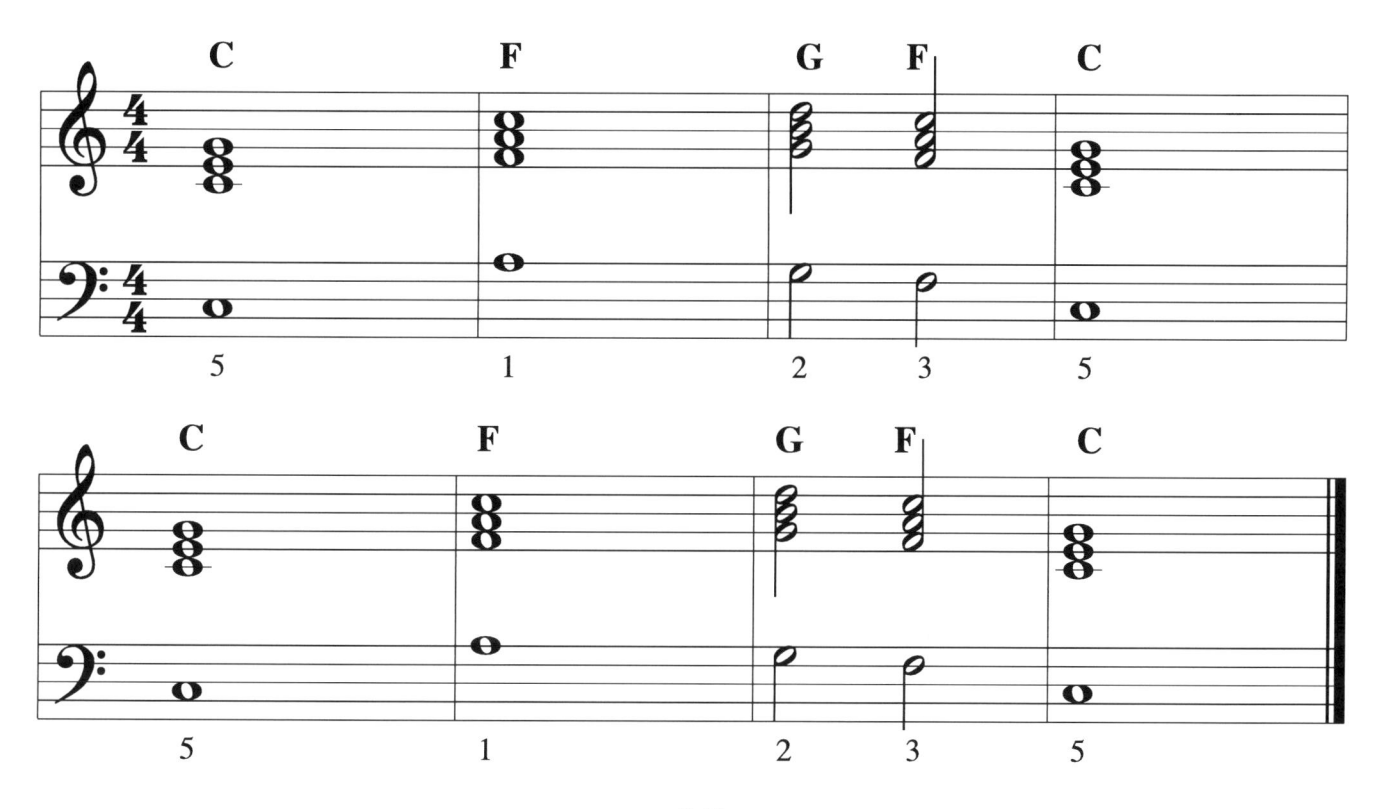

TOM DOOLEY

Use this very simple arrangement of *Tom Dooley* to practice your chords.

SECTION 4
C MAJOR SCALE

For Audio & Video Access, go to this internet address:
http://cvls.com/extras/keyboard/

THE C MAJOR SCALE

We can now learn our first scale. Scales are important because all the melodies and chords you hear in songs are derived from scales. The first scale you will learn is the C Major Scale. The C Major scale simply uses all the white keys on the keyboard, starting on C and ending on C.

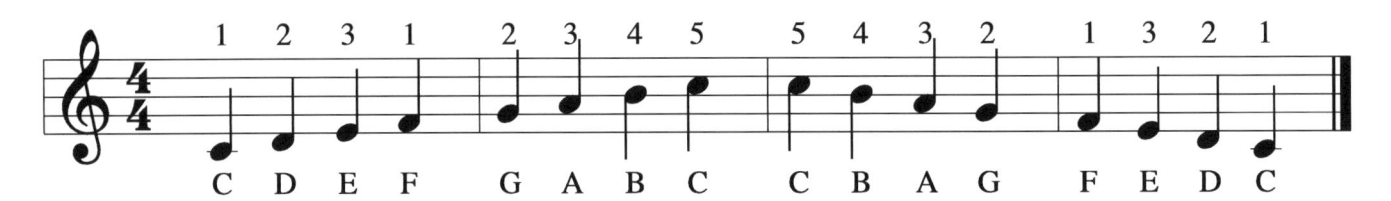

In order to play this scale with the right hand, you must first learn a new technique: crossing the thumb under the third finger.

1. Start with your thumb on middle C and play C, D, and E.

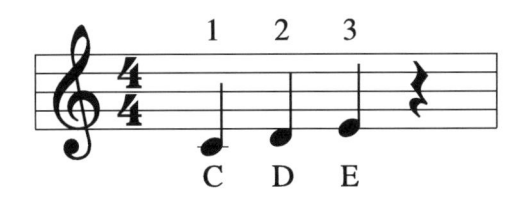

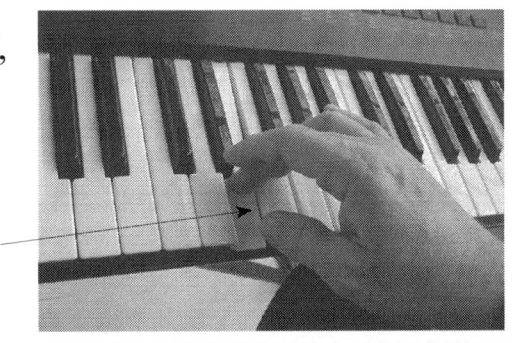

2. Cross your thumb under your 3rd finger and play F, G, A, B, and C.

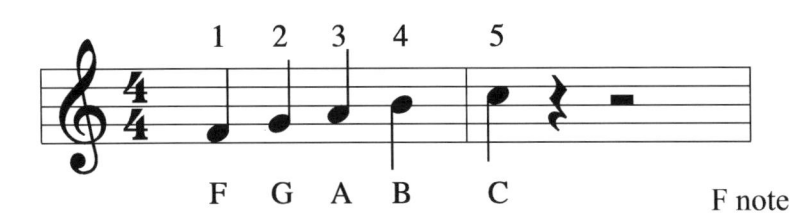

Thumb crossing under 3rd finger

EXERCISE 34

Play the C major scale forward with your right hand using this technique.

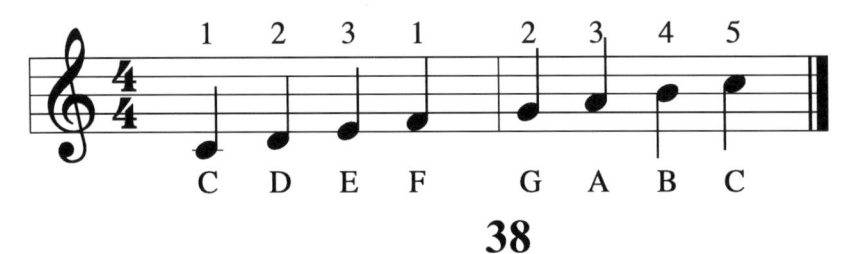

EXERCISE 35

1. Play the C Major Scale backwards, starting with your pinky on the note C - one octave higher than middle C. Play C, B, A, G, and F.

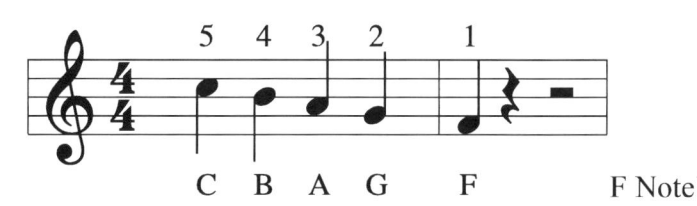

5 4 3 2 1
C B A G F

F Note

2. Cross your 3rd finger over your thumb and play E, D, and C.

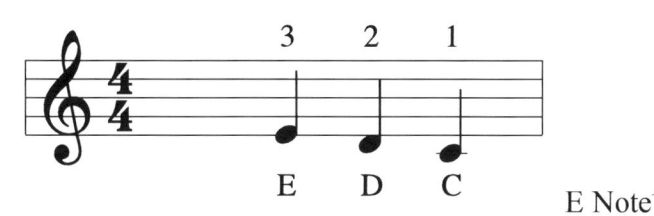

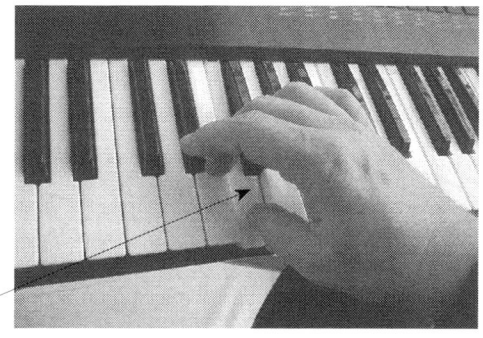

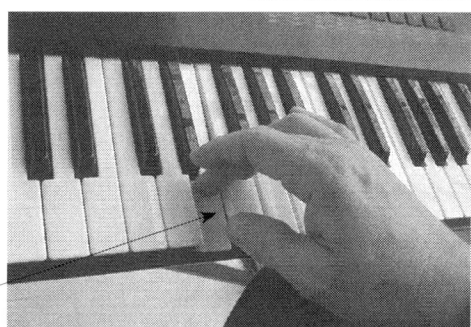

3 2 1
E D C

E Note

EXERCISE 36

Now play the C scale moving down the keyboard.

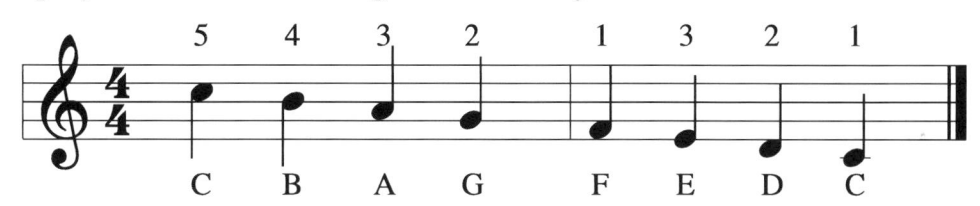

5 4 3 2 1 3 2 1
C B A G F E D C

EXERCISE 37

Practice the C Major Scale forward and backward, using the thumb cross technique you have just learned.

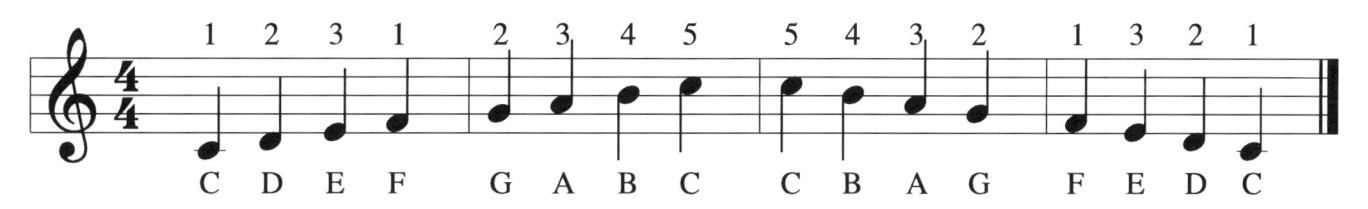

1 2 3 1 2 3 4 5 5 4 3 2 1 3 2 1
C D E F G A B C C B A G F E D C

EXERCISE 38

Here is a great exercise for working on the thumb cross. Practice this drill with your right hand over and over.

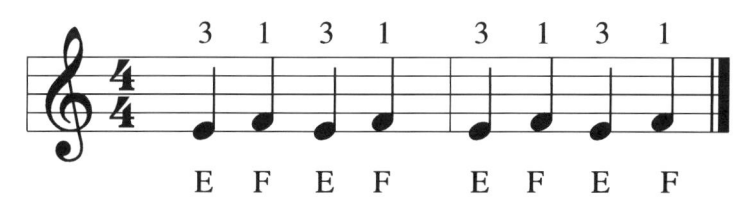

3 1 3 1 3 1 3 1
E F E F E F E F

C MAJOR SCALE /LEFT HAND

Let's play the C Major Scale using the left hand.

1. Start with your thumb on middle C and play C, B, and A.

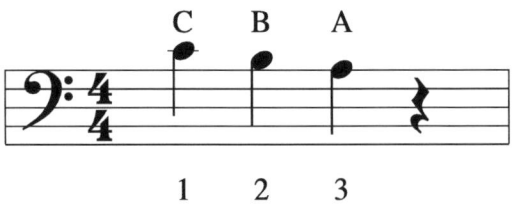

2. Cross your thumb under your third finger and play G, F, E, D, and C.

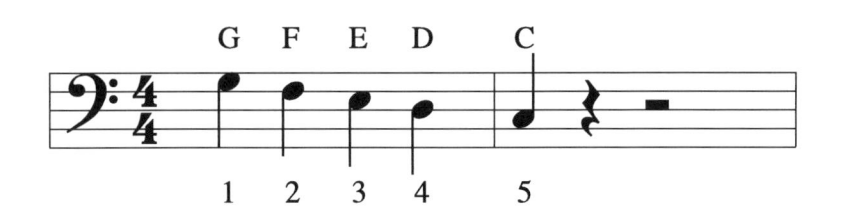

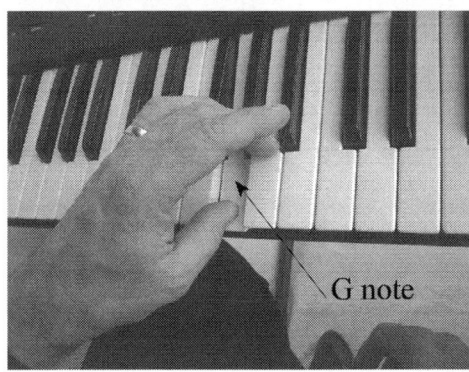

EXERCISE 39

Play the C Major Scale backwards with the left hand. Start on middle C, using the left thumb.

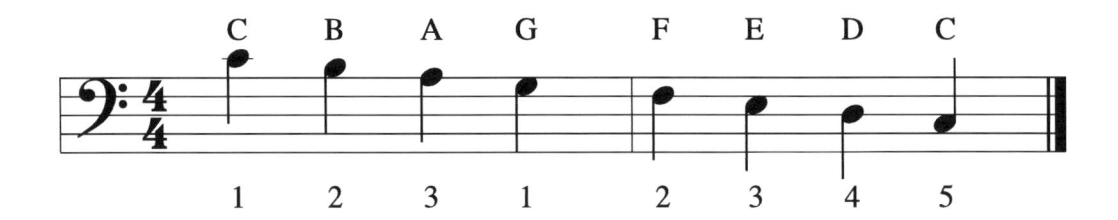

40

Now play the C Major scale forward starting with your left hand pinky on the note C, one octave below middle C.

1. Start with your pinky on the note C and play C, D, E, F, and G.

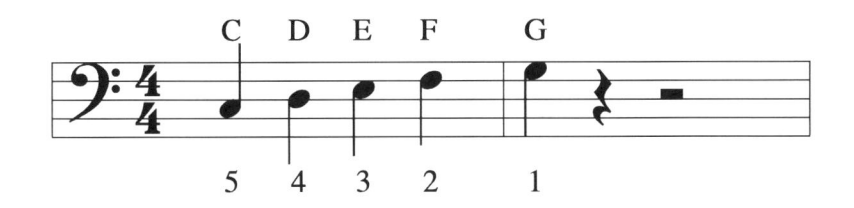

C D E F G
5 4 3 2 1

2. Cross your 3rd finger over your thumb and play A, B, and C.

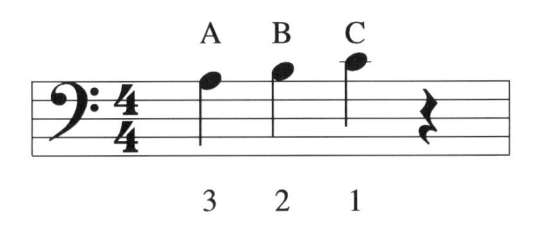

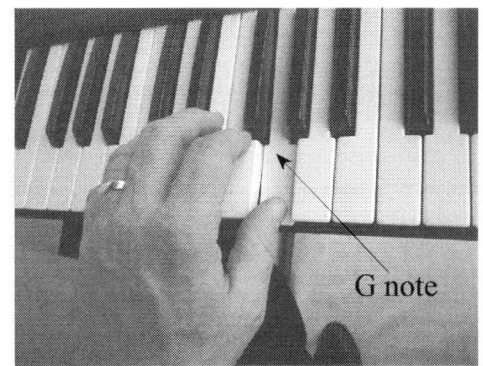

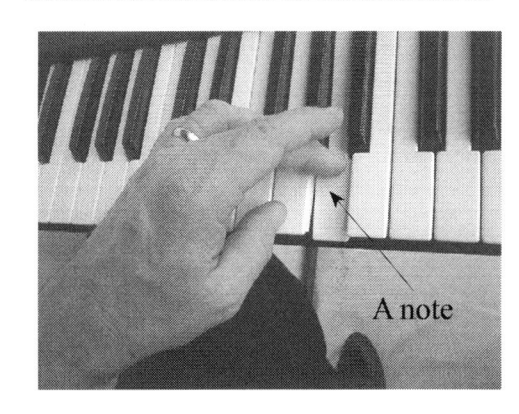

A B C
3 2 1

EXERCISE 40

Play the C Major Scale forward with your left hand, starting on the note C one octave below middle C. Use the technique you just learned.

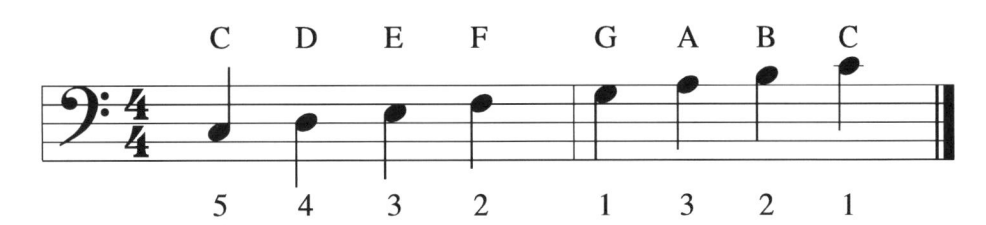

C D E F G A B C
5 4 3 2 1 3 2 1

EXERCISE 41

Let's try the cross over exercise using the left hand.

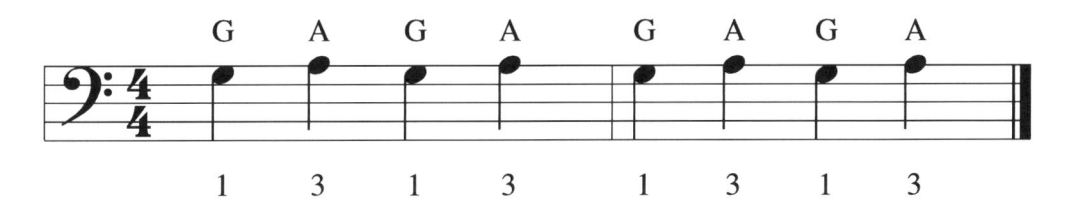

G A G A G A G A
1 3 1 3 1 3 1 3

C MAJOR SCALE SONG

We will now learn a song using the C Major Scale. This song is divided into 2 sections. It includes 8th notes, which are played twice the speed of quarter notes.

EXERCISE 42

Here's the right hand part to Section 1. Practice it until you are comfortable playing it.

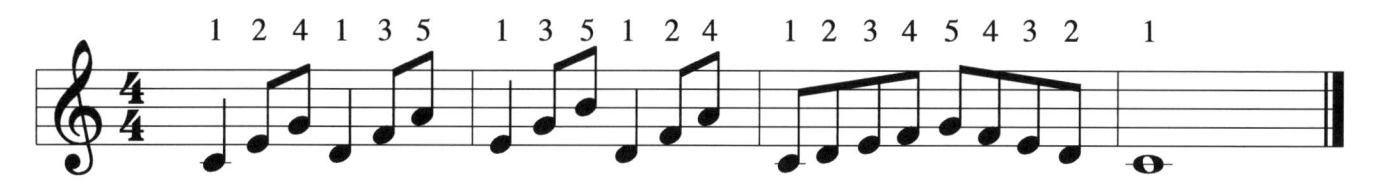

EXERCISE 43

Here's the right hand part to Section 2.

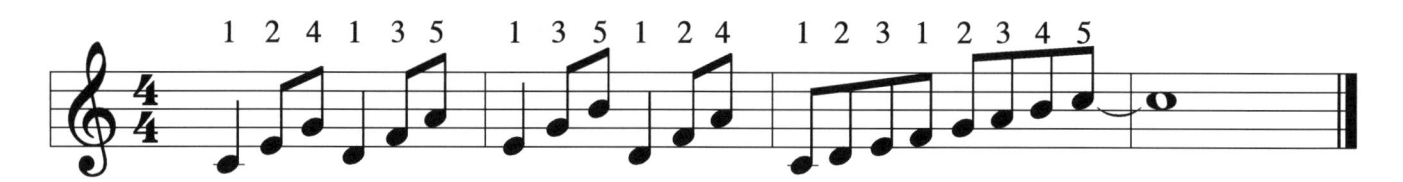

EXERCISE 44

Now practice Section 1, combining the left and right hand parts. Be patient and practice slowly and evenly.

42

EXERCISE 45

Now combine the right and left hand parts to Section 2.

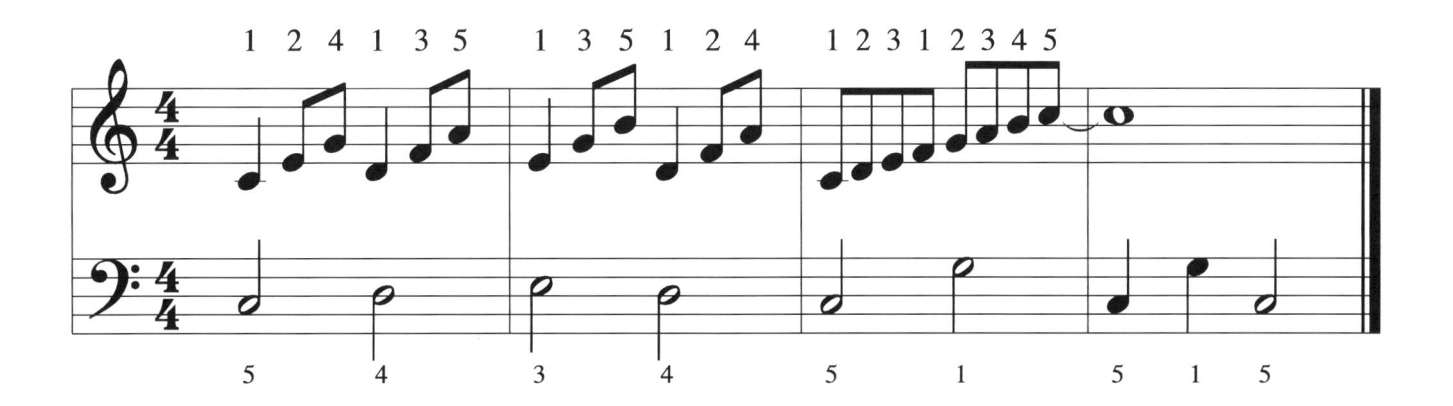

C MAJOR SONG

Now play the whole song. Practice slowly and evenly until it is smooth and easy, then speed it up and play the song with the band on the Video.

TWO HAND CONTROL

MICHAEL ROW THE BOAT ASHORE

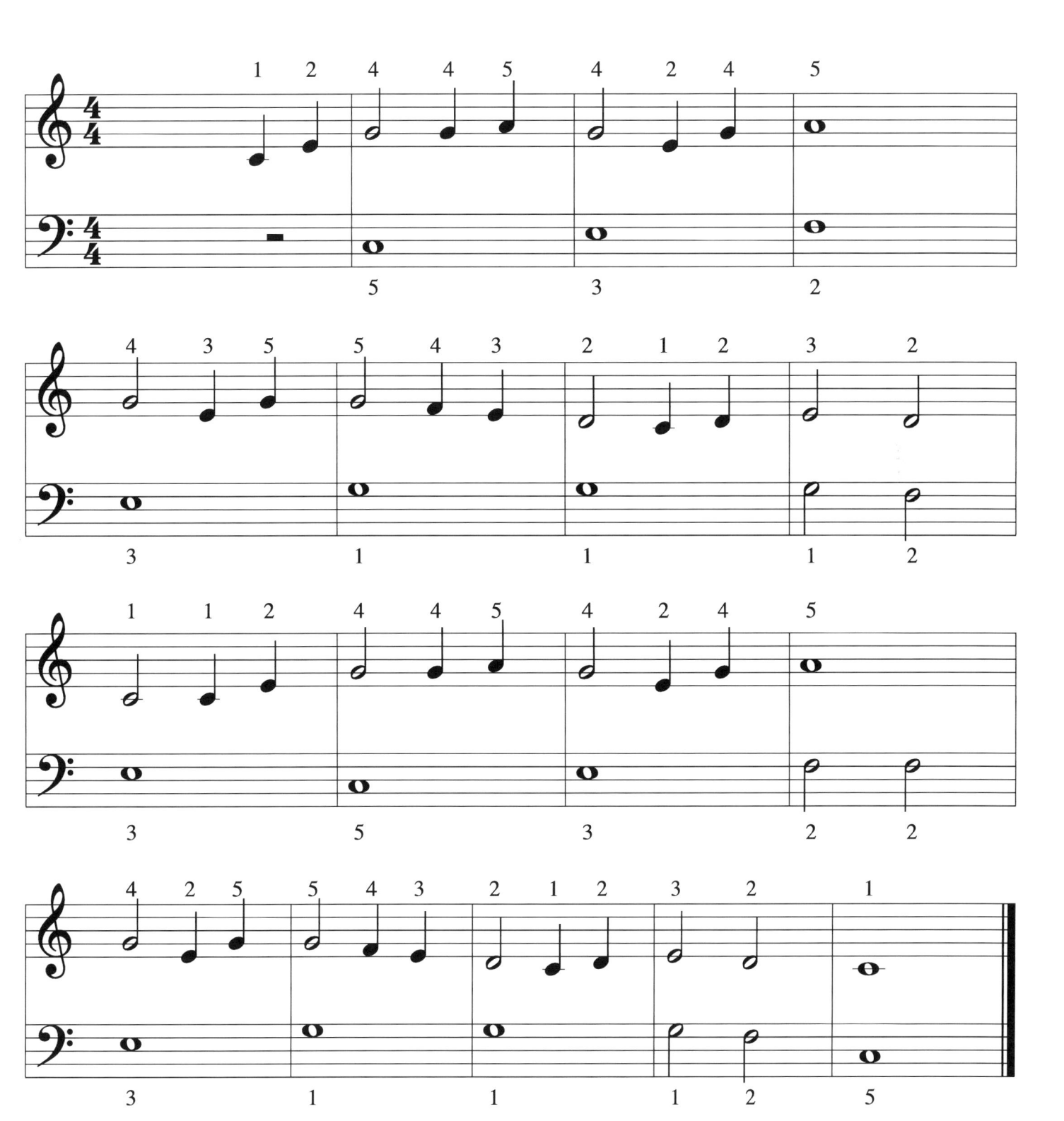

YANKEE DOODLE

OH SUZANNA

Practice your thumb crosses with this song.

THE CAISSONS GO ROLLING ALONG

49

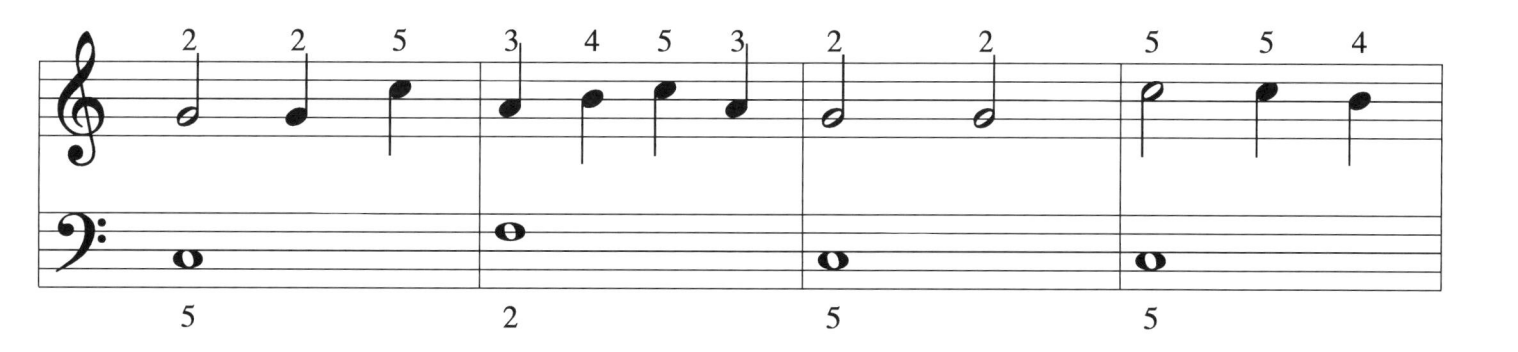

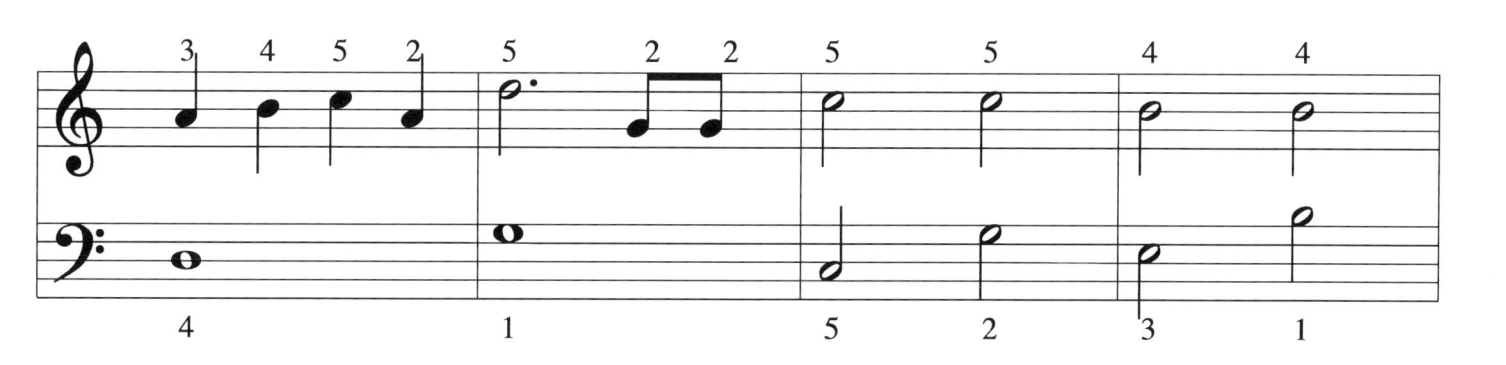

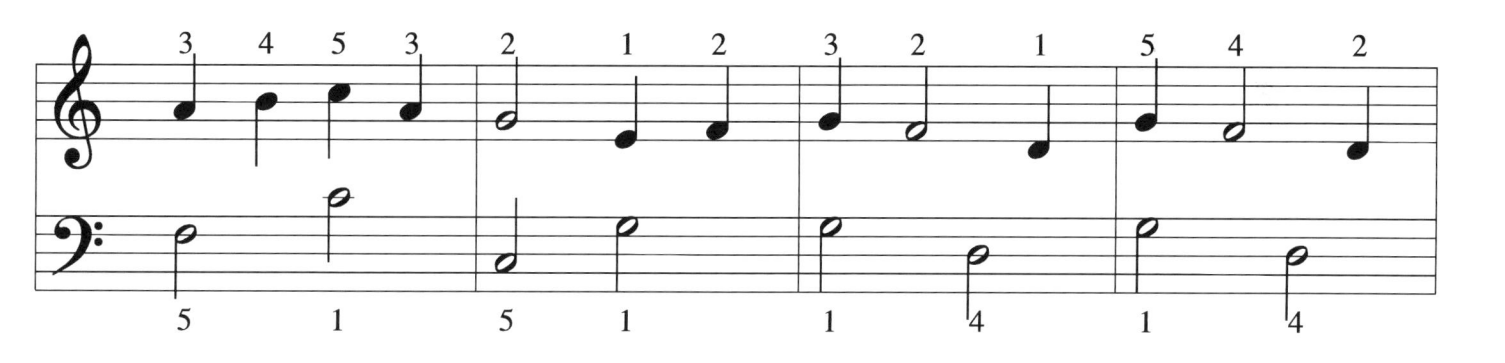

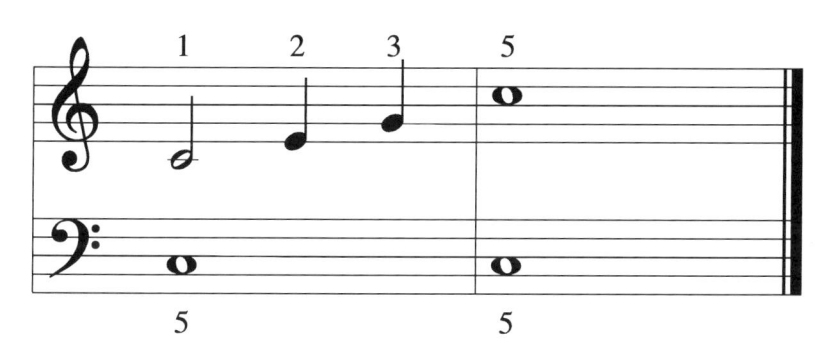

OH WHEN THE SAINTS

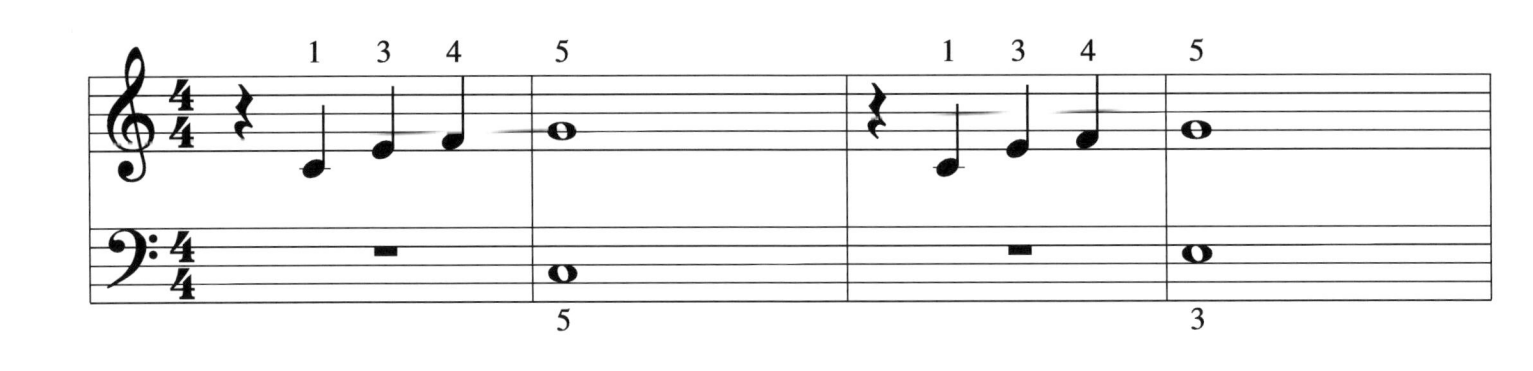

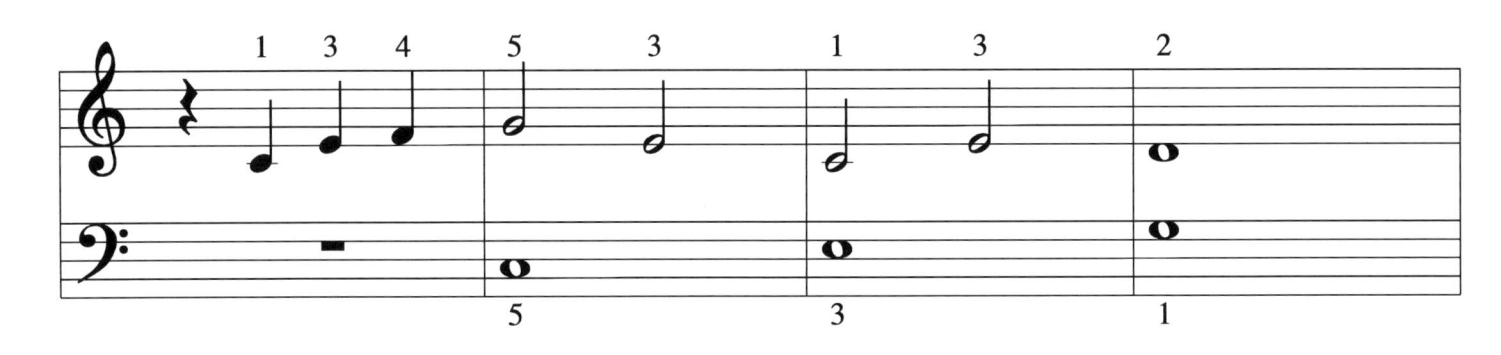

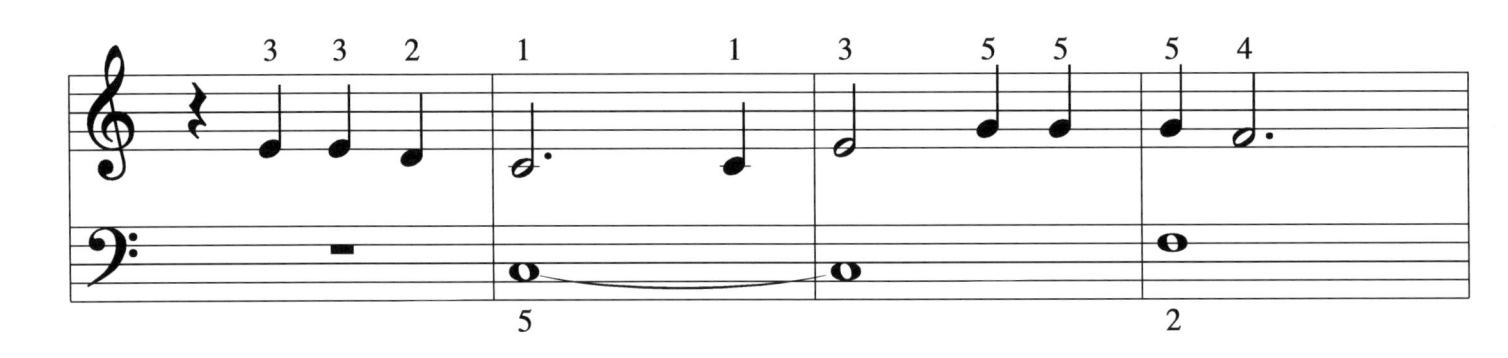

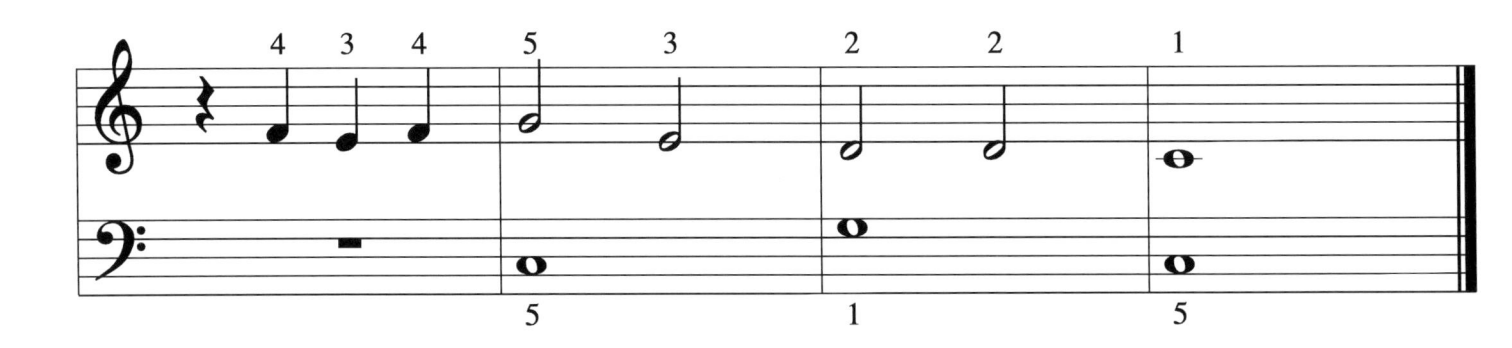

SCALING HEIGHTS

INTERVAL WORKOUT

TWINKLE, TWINKLE LITTLE STAR

CANON IN C

We're going to learn another song using the C Major Scale. This song is a bit more difficult, so practice slowly at first and then work on building speed. We will divide this song into four sections.

EXERCISE 46

Here is Section 1 with both the right and left hand parts. Pay close attention to the fingerings.

EXERCISE 47

Here is Section 2 with both the right and left hand parts.

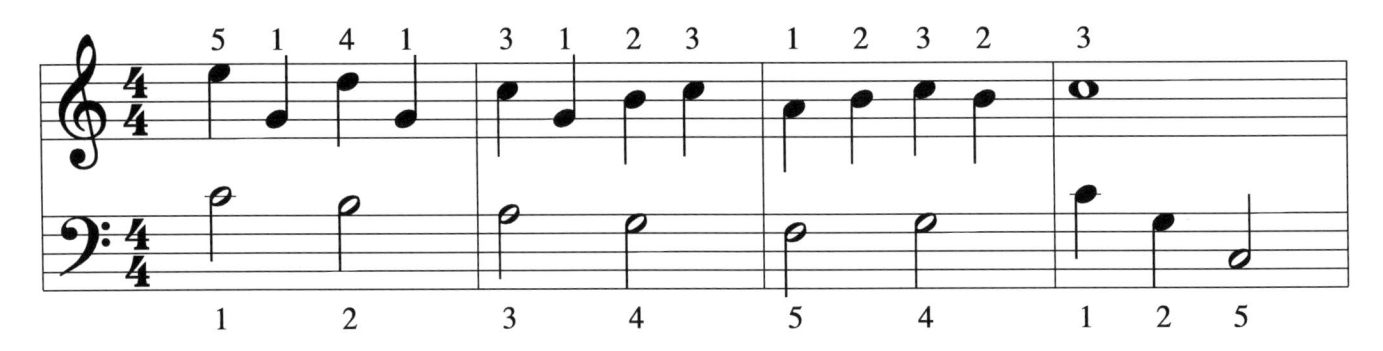

54

EXERCISE 48

Here is Section 3 with both the right and left hand parts.

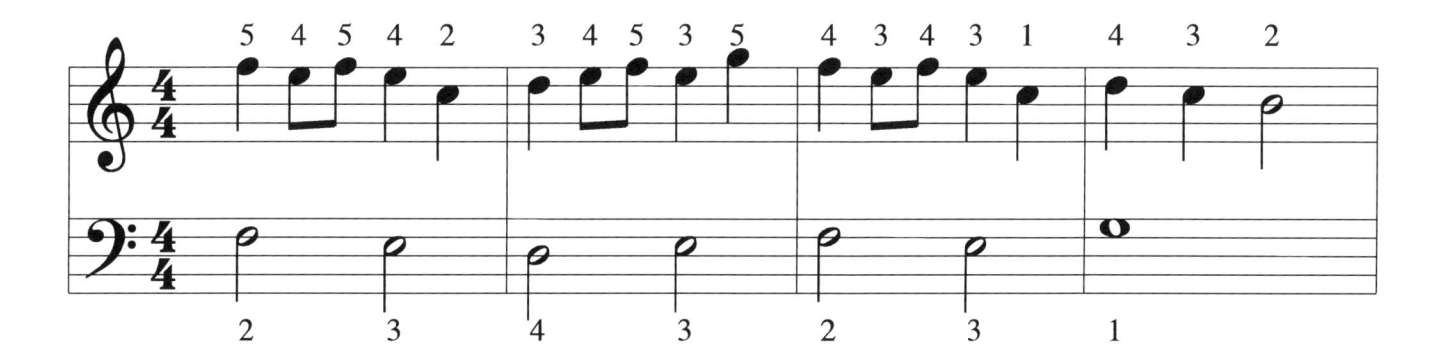

EXERCISE 49

Here is Section 4 with both the right and left hand parts.

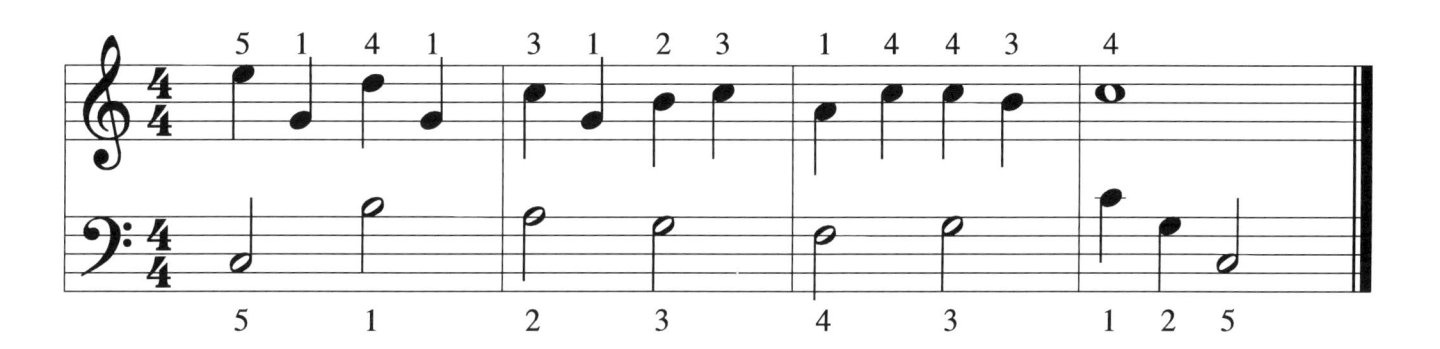

CANON IN C

Now practice the entire song. Remember to be patient and practice slowly and evenly. Pay special attention to the fingerings.

THIRDS

Made in the USA
San Bernardino, CA
04 August 2019